Llanfaethlu

1 Llys y Gwynt
2. Yr Efail Bach (Ty Mawr)
3. Glan y Gors.
4. Ty'n Pwll (demolished in the 1840's)
5. Ty Mawr (built in the 1840's)
6. Ty Mawr Mynydd
7. Plas Nico
8. Gors Goch
9. Ty Mawr Penrhosfeilw
10. Plas Meilw
11. Felin Heli
12. Tre Gof
13. Glangors Bach
14. St. Cybi's Church
15. Mynydd Gof Du
16. Glan yr Afon

Old Coach Road

Thomas Telford's New Road

Llanfihangel
yn Nhowyn

Tre feibion
Meurig

IN SEARCH OF ANGLESEY ANCESTRY

IN SEARCH OF
ANGLESEY ANCESTRY

Elizabeth Grace Roberts

PUBLISHED BY THE AUTHOR

1973:

*Published by H. E. G. Roberts, 25 Ballantrae Road,
Liverpool, and printed by Gwasg Gee, Denbigh.*

To my aunt

CATHERINE MARY BALLYN

who told me all the family stories

CONTENTS

INTRODUCTION

THIS climb up the family tree from the four grandparents became an absorbing occupation after my retirement, although our forebears had always been a source of great interest to us, even when we were children. Interest in our pedigree may be the result of more than a " trickle of Welsh blood " in our make-up. So many Welshmen can reel off a long line of descent from an ancestor who lived nearly three hundred years previously, naming the house, manor, or land from which this forebear sprang, and these claims prove to be authentic when examined.

Among the people described here is no one illustrious. It is their social backgrounds, so different between one branch and another, that interested us, and led my mother who was always fascinated by the lives of people of earlier days, to indulge in the wildest speculation and surmise, whenever there was a gap in our knowledge of our own people. What a great interest she would have taken in the recent search for how rewarding it has proved to be.

How much more is known about the forebears themselves from documents found during the search. There is one who in 1736 left one pound to each of his sons and the residue to his wife, Elizabeth; there is the great-grandfather whose draft will was found in my mother's old deed box. It reveals by every word, the trust and affection that had existed between his wife and himself for over fifty years. With this was found the simple affectionate letter written to his younger daughter just before her marriage. One of these forebears lived to be ninety, and as one of her older great-grandchildren I remember well how I listened to her reminiscences, soon becoming familiar with her pre-Victorian childhood. A great-aunt from another branch of the family also lived well on into her eighties, finally coming to make her home with us, bringing many of her possessions, and her tales were of a very different childhood.

The task of working backwards in time from these well known people was made easier by a fair collection of letters, documents, miniatures, photographs, and other personal possessions which have somehow survived, although their owners had moved from one end of the country to the other, more than once. The large old mahogany box which we always called my mother's deed box proved to have a most varied and unusual collection of papers some of which had been kept for sentimental or practical reasons. Others, surely had survived by mere chance, like the receipt for a ton of best coal which in 1876 had cost 16/-.

Each piece of china or glass, each article of furniture has its own story, from the small eighteenth century glass from which the great-aunt drank her nightly tot of whisky to the pretty little mug from which one grandmother, as a delicate child had been coaxed to drink milk drawn fresh from the cow, and so on to the silhouette of the great-great-great-grandfather who had become a follower of Swedenborg.

Perhaps the spur which urged on the search into the lives of all these people and gave me the wish to write an account of them was the interest shown in one particular branch of the family by two of my grandsons. Once the search began, the interest in what seemed at times to be the unravelling of a very tangled skein, carried me on. Information was gradually discovered which corroborated what was known, filled in gaps, turned fiction and surmise into facts, brought cold reality to bear on some of the family myths and legends, and provided one or two surprises.

Quite early in the search, four senior members of the family begged to be kept informed of any new discovery — the next piece in the large family jig-saw puzzle — and asked if they might contribute to the cost of the searches. Later, three of these four members of the club dropped out — perhaps they did not like what I was discovering. Soon after, two younger members of the family asked to join, so at regular intervals away goes the latest bulletin to Vancouver, Bath, and Worcestershire.

The original idea in writing about these people was to leave a record for the seven grandchildren and for any other younger members of the family who might care to have it. Even before sufficient material was collected, interested friends began to urge me to try to have the account published as a piece of genealogical research. This sounded a pretentious claim for a task which had given me such pleasure, excitement in my discoveries, some new cousins, one or two new friends, and visits to the 'ancestral' homes of some of the forebears — places in romantic and beautiful settings.

The first story to be completed, that of my Welsh paternal grandmother is primarily an exercise in genealogy. As I took each step upwards I felt I must weigh the evidence carefully and let my readers see on what facts, hunches or surmises I based my decisions. I was perhaps over cautious on certain occasions but also impetuous at times and made too-hasty decisions.

Inevitably I became fascinated by what I discovered, becoming interested in the people themselves. I was lucky to have access to the Papers of the Penrhos Estate at Bangor University from which I learned a good deal about the day to day occupations of my forebears. Towards the end, I realised that almost all the early farm tenants of the Penrhos family were my ancestors and very, very distant cousins — their connection with the Penrhos family covering a period of over two hundred and fifty years, and even today, one of the former Penrhos houses is owned and occupied by a member of the Hughes family. I have not attempted to show all these people on the pedigree, because many of the connections are those made by marriages in the distant past, some as long ago as 1750.

It has all taken a very long time, nearly six years; this was partly because I pursued the forebears of my maternal grandparents at the same time. But the work and research involved has been absorbing.

11

For the work on the Anglesey kinsmen, I owe very much to the interest, help and encouragement of my friend John Bulmer who lent me one of his transcriptions of the Holyhead Parish Registers. These were invaluable when I was working at home. I am also indebted to him for finding two marriages in his transcriptions of the Llanfaethlu and Llanfihangel-yn-Nhowyn Registers and for looking up several Census Returns at the Public Record Office. I am grateful to the Rev. Canon D. T. Davies, Rector of Holyhead, who allowed me to search in his registers during periods when I was at Holyhead. I owe a good deal to Mr. Dewi O. Jones, Anglesey County Librarian and Archivist, for his many helpful letters, and to Mr. A. Giles Jones, Archivist at the University College of North Wales, for his interest and help, whenever I was working on the Penrhos Papers. I am indebted to Mr. B. G. Owens, Keeper of Records and Manuscripts at the National Library of Wales, for making searches in Bishops' Transcripts and sending me copies of wills. Mr. A. Maldwyn Jones, Public Health Inspector at Holyhead has been unfailingly helpful in locating long vanished streets and buildings in Holyhead, and in advising me where to look for certain information. I am also very grateful to Mr. Ellis C. Williams, Headmaster of the Thomas Ellis Primary School who gave me access to the Log Books of the old National School. My numerous cousins, first, second and third have willingly and patiently answered all the searching questions put to them and for this, I should like to thank them. To my newly-discovered distant cousins, or more precisely my third cousins once removed, — Freda Beck Jones and Trevor Lloyd, I am grateful for giving me their pedigrees, one of which corroborated all I had found and gave me the clue to the first two forebears, and the other which neatly fitted on to my own stem as a collateral branch.

To my aunt, Catherine Ballyn, I owe most of all. In her keeping are so many of the letters, photographs, and silhouettes which have helped me in my work. Every time I saw her she would bring from the depths of her memory, some fresh piece of information which fitted neatly on to one branch of the tree. She passed on all the family stories and insisted on relationships which I finally, with one exception, proved to be real ones. I am not without hope that eventually the missing relationship will be proved[1] though exactly where I can fit it in among these closely packed names, I do not know.

I owe many others gratitude for their interest and for their endless patience with my hobby horse which, on the many occasions I have mounted it, galloped for hours on end.

ELIZABETH GRACE ROBERTS.

Liverpool.
June, 1973.

[1] See Appendix A for the solution to the mystery.

CHAPTER 1

Our Hughes family of Holyhead

THIS pedigree was traced backwards from my paternal grandmother, Grace Ballyn, born Hughes in 1852.

At first it was a very slender family tree with a few side branches bearing the names of people known to the generation immediately before my own. By the time I seriously began this search, there remained only three persons of this earlier generation, my father's younger sister and brother, and one of their first cousins. Because my aunt was almost the youngest of her generation, her own memory of people and incidents went no farther back than about 1890, but she has handed on to me a rich store of information handed down from her mother, Grace. On these stories I have based my search, finding evidence of their truth in the Holyhead Parish Registers, from Somerset House, from Census Returns, from the wills of these forebears, and only one relationship have I so far failed to trace, that between ourselves and Hugh Hugh Hughes. He has always been accepted by my father's generation as the uncle of Grace. But the Welsh are often vague about relationships. They are aware of them but usually refer to a kinsman of the same generation as a cousin, never a first or second cousin, and a kinsman of an earlier generation is called an uncle or aunt, though the kinsman may in fact be a cousin once or twice removed.

Hugh Hugh Hughes was born in Holyhead in 1844, and died in Lower Bebington, Cheshire, in 1887. Amongst other legacies, he left £10,000 to form a trust, the income from

15

which was to be given "towards the maintenance or relief of poor or necessitous persons either male or female and without reference to their religious belief or creed, resident within the parish of Holyhead, in the county of Anglesey". The testator himself was a staunch Churchman. I have discovered a good deal about Hugh himself and his immediate forebears, but not the supposed connection between us. He cannot therefore appear on this pedigree.

My aunt gradually became as interested as I in the search, and as we talked, she recalled people and incidents long since forgotten. These I noted down as they were told to me, and almost always these recollections would help to fill in gaps in the huge jig-saw puzzle. I'm afraid, too, that I sometimes laid traps for my aunt, as on the afternoon when I had returned from a solitary walk. On being asked where I had been, I described the route I had followed, deliberately mentioning the name of a little farm, Yr Efail Bach. After my latest search in the parish registers, I had become convinced that one of our forebears was living there at the beginning of the 19th century. Later on that evening, my aunt suddenly said, "We are related to the people of Yr Efail Bach." I have since proved her to be correct, but look at the pedigree and marvel at the long racial memory. In the 18th century, this small-holding was called Ty Mawr, and together with Llys-y-gwynt was farmed by William Hughes who appears near the top of the pedigree. When this William died in 1810, the tenancy of Ty Mawr, now called Yr Efail Bach, was granted to his grandson, another William who was associated with the place for over sixty years. So this particular recollection of my aunt's had been handed down from the middle of the last century, probably even earlier.

So many Welshmen can, if asked, reel off verbally a long line of descent, giving the house or farm from which they spring or naming a poet, preacher or other well-known person from whom they have descended. This descent, upon examination proves to be accurate. Before the Tudors ascended the English throne, Wales still had her own laws, framed by Hywel Dda (Howel the Good) in the eleventh century. These in some respects were more enlightened than those prevailing in England, particularly those relating to marriage and the rights of women. The laws of land tenure in Wales had prevailed from even earlier times, — the law of Gavelkind whereby land and property descended in equal shares among the children.

All this I had learned many years previously but now I realised as never before how some of the Welsh character had been moulded by these ancient tribal laws. Some of their attributes are amusing, exasperating or inexplicable to the Englishman. The so-called clannishness had been bred in them from time immemorial. This long memory of the pedigree, essential if a man were to claim his rightful share of the tribal land still persists today. I was soon to discover that in many wills of the 17th, 18th and 19th centuries money and property is often left in absolutely equal shares among all the children. However, I am digressing, and must return to Grace Hughes.

As Grace, my grandmother was originally the corner-stone of this now very large edifice, an attempt should perhaps be made to set down my own recollections of her and her household between the years 1907 and 1916, the year she died.

CHAPTER 2

Memories of Rostrevor, Holyhead, 1907-1911

WHEN one is a very small child, houses seem to be almost as important as people who live in them. Of one house, Rostrevor, near the top of Station Street in Holyhead, and of my frequent visits there in the years before 1911, I still retain a vivid memory. Rostrevor was the home of my paternal grandparents — a double-fronted house with a narrow strip of garden enclosed by a low wall surmounted by railings. The large bushes of Veronica which flourished each side of the door were fascinating, for each closed pair of leaves could be opened to reveal a smaller pair which in turn were opened to reveal yet another pair. This game I often played until protests about injury to the bushes made me desist. The interior of the house had its own particular smell — a very pleasant one, very difficult to analyse and describe. I now imagine that it was a scent compounded of several agreeable things like beeswax, freshly-ironed linen, the cooking of delicious food, and sometimes a very faint smell of tobacco smoke. All these smells I must have known at home, but at Rostrevor I was more aware of them in a very pleasurable way. Here I arrived, sometimes for convalescence after illness, and at least once just before the arrival of a new baby at home.

At this time, seven people were living at Rostrevor. Of the two youthful uncles, I have not many clear pictures. The younger one, Harry, was still at school. He seemed a big teasing boy to me, a larger edition of the brother at home who was also a tease. Even vaguer memories remain of the

18

uncle who was called Wyndham. He always appeared immaculate and did not like any tempestuous behaviour which might rumple his clothes. I learned later that he had been rather a dandy when at this age.

Of my grandfather I saw very little, as I was usually in bed when he returned home in the evenings. I remember that he was handsome, that he reminded me of King Edward VIIth, and that his beard tickled my cheek when he kissed me. He had a beautiful voice, and often called me Gypsy. I also knew that he spoke French fluently, but had no Welsh. He always gave me three pennies every Saturday — vast riches in those days.

The two aunts, Pauline and Catherine were very important to me, especially the younger aunt whose name I was never able to pronounce when I was very small, so I called her Dodo, not Catherine. This became Do, as the years passed, and to our family this well-loved aunt is still Do, though to our cousins she is Aunt Catherine.

Aunt Pauline was very dark. I never remember such blue-black hair, and in those days hair was not tinted. Her hair was very thick and straight, worn with a centre parting, and brushed smoothly back. I was occasionally awake to see the nightly ritual practised by both aunts, when hair was brushed until it shone. Aunt Pauline had dark brown eyes and an olive skin, and an admirably straight nose. I also remember that she had beautiful hands. Looking at early photographs of her, I now realise she was a very beautiful woman.

Aunt Do always made me think of a very beautiful gentle, grey dove. In appearance, she was a complete contrast to her sister. Her hair was light brown, her skin fair and her eyes grey. In those days she was to me the most important person in that house — always kind, loving and patient. Looking back, I now realise that it was a lively, often naughty and sometimes tiresome small niece who usually shared Aunt Do's bedroom during those visits to Holyhead. These sleeping arrangements were to me, of course, very pleasurable and poor Aunt Do was invariably awakened at

19

six each morning, with a request for a story. If she pretended to be asleep, I would climb into her bed and try to raise her eyelids, saying, " Are you awake, Aunty Dodo? " And never was she cross, and always there was a story. Sometimes they were fairy stories and occasionally they were stories about myself, when I was almost a baby. The one I remember most vividly is of an incident which must have taken place before I was three. At that time we were living in Holyhead, and I was often taken with my brother, Clifford, in our mail cart (a wicker-work carriage in which we sat back to back) as far as the Holyhead Breakwater. I was fascinated by and rather afraid of the noisy engine which pulled trucks of stones quarried from the mountain, along the length of the Breakwater. So impressed was I by the size of this monster and by the alarming noise it made that I always called it a Thunder-Scatter. This was a story I liked to hear, although at the age of seven I always felt pity for the very little girl and slightly scornful about her fear of the engine which now appeared to me nothing more than a toy engine.

I was Aunty Do's shadow. We went to church together, to the market, to the beach, and as I grew older, I sometimes accompanied her to the National School where she taught the infants. She taught in that school for forty-five years and I often tease her that she must have hundreds of old pupils in Holyhead. Indeed she is often greeted by people, strangers to me whom on enquiry prove to be old pupils of hers.

To us, our Welsh grandmother was Nina Ballyn, and this title was always used by us. The Welsh word for grandmother is, of course, Nain, but this we never used. I think perhaps my English great-grandmother Ballyn elected to be called Nina by her grandchildren, for my aunts invariably addressed their grandmother as Nina, and we perhaps adopted the title for our grandmother, using the term old Nina, for our great-grandmother Ballyn! In retrospect, the latter term now sounds highly disrespectful.

My grandmother Ballyn is remembered as dark, pretty, energetic, kind, but sometimes brusque, as well she might be, for I was often naughty. She used terms of endearment which at that time I did not understand, "Del", "Cariad", and "Mi'r wyt ti'n dlws". Though the words were incomprehensible, I knew by her smile and by the tone of her voice that I was in favour. I loved to hang around her in the big kitchen in Rostrevor, to watch what was going on. There are recollections of an enormous pan mug, as it was called, in which the dough was set to rise, or in which batter was mixed for "crempog", or ingredients for bara-brith. This delicious bara-brith would be sliced thinly and buttered. There were also large egg custards in pastry and these were always baked in very large brown rectangular pie-dishes, as were the delectable fruit pies. I can also remember large joints of beef roasting in front of a bright clear fire. My grandfather would carve thin slices of this, and using a large gravy spoon, would fill it with what he called "blue" gravy which had run from the joint, and pour it over my vegetables. I often wondered why he called what was obviously red gravy, "blue". Perhaps he was translating literally the term "saignant bleu".

At the back of Rostrevor was a garden, and when I was there on a long visit, I had a tiny garden of my own in which I usually planted mignonette seeds. I never see mignonette grown now.

An ancient doll's perambulator was brought down from one of the attics and the very docile tabby cat, Tiddles, was dressed in an old-fashioned doll's cape and bonnet. She lay placidly on her back in the perambulator her forepaws resting on the coverlet, while I wheeled her around the garden!

But there were other rather naughty activities. On one occasion a large number of snails were placed one after another, within a large pipe protruding from the back of the house, near the ground. This appeared to me to be a mysterious tunnel. It was made of thick brown earthenware, and the snails moved along this into the unknown darkness. Where it led, I did not know, but the following Monday morning, when Aunt Pauline removed the lid of the copper in the wash-house to fill it ready for washing day, she saw a large collection of snails at the bottom of the copper!

In the garden I can also remember gooseberry and black-currant bushes and that on the gooseberry bushes I tore a large rent in the sleeve of a new dress that my mother had recently made for me. I was a tomboy and loved to climb trees and slide down rocks of which there were any number in the neighbourhood. The resulting damage to the white starched knickers and long black woollen stockings which I, like all little girls at that time invariably wore, must have added considerably to the work on washing day, and to the pile of mending in the sewing basket. But these sins were soon forgiven, and the next time I appeared in the kitchen, "feeling hungry", would be given some tit-bit from the larder. One of these was often a small piece of home-made bread spread with salty Welsh butter and sprinkled with Demerara sugar. The Welsh name for this particular delicacy has long since been forgotten, but not the flavour of the mouthful.

Nina Ballyn always seemed to be in that kitchen, pre-paring meals, helped by Aunt Pauline. Perhaps she sat with her hands in her lap, after I had gone to bed. I know that she usually went to Welsh Evensong on Sundays and often to a Welsh week-night service.

When she went away with my grandfather, it was usually to visit one of her married sons, living in Chester, Stony Stratford and Liverpool. Sometimes she went alone, returning to Holyhead accompanied by a grandchild on a visit. While she was making one of these visits to us in Liverpool, Edward VIIth died, and the two events are linked in my memory. There was much talk about the royal funeral and the visiting kings and queens who would be in the country for the occasion. I was impressed by Nina's knowledge of the royal family relationships. My most vivid recollection of the pictures I saw is of the King's dog, Caesar, walking in the funeral procession.

22

Soon after this there was the excitement of a return visit to Holyhead, with Nina, this time for a long stay, as I had not been well and the Anglesey air would be beneficial. There was the thrill of a journey on the Irish Mail train, the pleasure of being with Nina, the looking forward to seeing Aunt Do. We joined the Irish Mail at Chester, and from there travelled swiftly to Holyhead in ninety minutes, on this long train drawn by two engines. How different today, when after a two hours' wait at Chester one boards an undistinguished train of perhaps two coaches, with a diesel engine. The arrival at Holyhead was also exciting in those days for there was a great bustle, and most of the passengers would be joining the boat for Ireland. The Station Master wore a frock coat and silk hat and always had a flower in his buttonhole. The excitement of the journey is still clear in my memory, and the looking forward to being at Rostrevor. This, although I did not know it, was to be my last visit to the house.

The seventh inhabitant of Rostrevor was hardly known to me at that time, though I came to know her very well a year or two later. She was " old " Nina, my grandfather's mother, so called to distinguish her from Nina, my grandmother. At that time she would be eighty-seven, and seemed to me very, very old. She had her own sitting room, and I was not encouraged to enter this very often. When we did meet, I always felt rather subdued by the piercing blue eyes turned upon me. I was also fascinated by her erect figure and the black lace cap which covered the top of her head. Old Nina seemed to have a life of her own, apart from the family. All her friends were English, and Nina's were Welsh. Any member of the household going in to talk to old Nina did so alone, and I supposed this was because of her extreme old age. I knew that Aunty Do spent most of her evenings in old Nina's sitting room, when she was preparing for examinations and she was often there when I had gone to bed, but it was not until the year following my last visit to Rostrevor that I came to know old Nina well.

On May Day, 1911, Nina Ballyn was in the garden. There had been heavy rain but the sun was now shining and there were some clothes to be pegged on the line. Nina's foot slipped on a wet paving stone and she fell heavily, breaking her leg. After one or two days in bed she was restless and not sleeping well. It was decided that my grandfather should sleep in the spare room, so that they should not disturb one another.

The house was lit by gas, but each person carried a candlestick with a lighted candle, when upstairs at night, to light the way along the landing or up to the top floor. My grandfather had been in to say goodnight to Nina and had been told to " be careful with the candle " and to " be sure to put it out." He laughed and said he would eat it. Later, on leaving his bedroom to go to the bathroom, he turned as usual to go along the landing, forgetting he was not in his own bedroom. He went headlong down the stairs which were a yard from the door of the spare bedroom. The doctor was summoned immediately; the fall had broken his neck and he died within two hours.

He was sixty-four and his wife sixty. Life at Rostrevor came to an end. The one uncle still at home went to sea, making his home with us when he was ashore. Nina Ballyn, old Nina, and the two aunts went to live in a much smaller house. Old Nina no longer had her own sitting room but shared the big living room with the other three members of the family. And in this house Do is still living.

Nina never really recovered from the shock of my grandfather's death. She grieved and blamed herself for the accident. Why had she allowed him to go to another bedroom? Her doctor said this reaction was partly due to her enforced inactivity at the time of the tragedy. Had she been able to do something and share in all the sad affairs that followed her husband's death, she would have been physically exhausted and would have had less time to dwell on what had happened.

She was a sad little figure now. She seemed to me to shrink and become tiny, her dark eyes seemed too large and full of grief. She gradually relinquished the housekeeping to her elder daughter and lived in her own sad world, dying in 1916 at the age of sixty-four.

CHAPTER 3

Parentage, childhood and marriage of Grace Hughes

FROM no one in the family could I gain a picture of William Hughes, father of my grandmother, Grace. If only I had been able to begin this search earlier, when my father was still alive. He was nine and a half years older than Aunt Do and could have told me so much more of those early days. I did learn that William when on shore used to visit his daughter, Grace and her family, when Do was a very small child. He wore a short dark blue, double-breasted reefer jacket and smoked a pipe. Do remembers him as a handsome and happy person. The only possession of his still in existence is a book of family prayers given to him by his sister, Ann Grace, soon after his fourth daughter was born.

William Hughes was a mariner, and married the daughter of a mariner, John Roberts, whose wife, Margaret Bell came from Cheshire. Mariners are often a source of great trouble to the genealogist, professional or amateur. In those early days, there were thriving ports all round the coasts of this island where a mariner might find his bride. He might settle in her town or village near the coast, or bring her home to his native place. So far, I have failed to find a record of the marriage of John Roberts and Margaret, though the baptisms of all their children are in the Holyhead parish registers. We, as children heard of Margaret Bell, and my mother possessed a small ivory pencil which had once belonged to her.

John and Margaret's elder daughter was Mary Roberts, born in 1826, and she and William Hughes, mariner, were married in the parish church, Holyhead, on July 19th, 1847.

26

Only recently, my sister gave me a very faded testimonial, or reference as it would be called in those days. The double sheet of writing paper has a small embossed crest of three feathers, at the top left-hand corner, though there is no motto. The double sheet is folded and on the outside is written, Mary Roberts, Holyhead. The testimonial reads as follows: " Mary Roberts lived with me for one year and nine months during which time she behaved herself soberly, honestly and quietly. She understands washing and needle-work remarkably well. She is now discharged at her own request, having first paid (sic) her all wages due."

The signature is M. E. Browne, the name of the house is almost undecipherable and is preceded by the words Belle Vue, Booterstown. It is dated June 29th, 1847. If I can decipher the address, it may prove to be in the parish from which Mary's mother, Margaret Bell, came. She had perhaps sent her daugher, Mary, as a nurse-maid to a family near her old home, in Cheshire. It would be splendid if a little successful detective work produced another marriage for the main stem of the pedigree.

Mary Roberts was, of course, returning home to Holyhead for her marriage to William Hughes, three weeks later.

The eldest daughter of William and Mary Hughes was Mary, born in June 1848. From her birth certificate, we find them living in the area known as Black Bridge, then the eastern side of a deep indentation which was a beach in those days. The shore of this bay was cut in two at its head by the little river known as Afon Trip, and across this, above the high water mark was built the bridge called Bont Ddu, or Black Bridge. A row of houses fringed the eastern shore and many of them still stand today in the road known as Black Bridge. From the parish registers we find that they were mostly occupied by mariners or those whose work was connected with the sea. By 1856, the river had been covered over and the Black Bridge itself had gone. About 1865, a bridge was built to carry the main road — the last lap of Telford's road which we now call the A5, over the railway.

The railway had been finished in 1848 and its terminus was by 1854 on the western side of the shore. The whole of this shore, of course, disappeared in the 1870's when land was reclaimed, and the new deep harbour was made, but Nina Ballyn had told me she remembered this area when it was still a shore, and she a small child.

When William Hughes's second daughter, Margaret, arrived in December 1849, the little family was living in one of the newly-built houses in London Road. Grace followed Margaret in January 1852, and Ann in 1854, the family now living in Station Place.[2] From the rental lists among the Penrhos Papers, I found William Hughes paying ground rent of £2 per annum, to the Penrhos Estate.

In 1856, William's wife, Mary died, soon after the death of her fifth child, a son named Thomas, who died when seven months old. She was just over thirty and William was left with four very young daughters. He never re-married, giving his two elder girls, Mary and Margaret, into the care of his sister, Ann Grace Hughes, who for a short time had a small private school near St. Cybi's Church in the house known as Quiet Corner.

Quite recently I was able to visit the house Quiet Corner which is next to a much larger house once occupied by Captain Skinner,[3] and until 1810 Quiet Corner was rented by Captain William Goddard[4] who soon after that date retired, and went to live outside the town at Llys-y-gwynt, but in the 1860's, this pretty little house was occupied by Miss Goddard.

Quiet Corner just over a hundred years ago must have been a very pleasant house. The rooms are surprisingly spacious with large sash windows looking out from the back over what was then a quiet harbour with its beach almost at the foot of the garden behind the house. The large kitchen and the equally big schoolroom above would be flooded with

[2] Now known as Old Station.
[3] Penrhos Rental Lists.
[4] Penrhos Rental Lists.

28

sunshine on a sunny morning. There is no garden in front of the house which faces west, but its position is secluded and even today it could be a delightful home. It is now, alas. a shop and its pretty façade has gone.

When questioning Do about this school, I learned that my maternal grandmother, Ellen Hall, had been a pupil there for a short time after 1853 when the Halls moved from the lighthouse at St. Ann's Head, Pembrokeshire, and settled in Holyhead, John Hall becoming Principal Lightkeeper at the Skerries Lighthouse. What a strange coincidence that Ann Grace Hughes should teach the child whose daughter was later in 1900 to marry my father, William Ballyn, great nephew of Ann Grace herself.

Ellen Hall also touches this story in another way. Her parents, John and Elizabeth Hall, became the friends of John Bulmer's[5] grandparents, John and Ann Hughes of Castle House, Stanley Crescent. This friendship was broken by the deaths of John and Elizabeth Hall in 1881 and 1884, but their elder daughter, Elizabeth Greenough, maintained the connection till she finally left Holyhead in 1907.

There was a renewal of this link between descendants of these Hughes and the Halls in 1917, when my eldest brother, Clifford, became a friend of John Bulmer's eldest brother, Kenneth. And only a few years ago John Bulmer and I met and continued the association, soon after I discovered the signatures of John's grandfather and uncle, John and Thomas Griffith Hughes on my great-grandfather Hall's draft will.

This digression has led me away from my Welsh story.

Grace and Ann, the younger children of the widowed mariner, William Hughes, went to excellent foster partents, Richard and Ann Jones, then living at 3 Mill Street. In the 1861 Census Returns, the two little girls aged nine and seven appear at this address. Soon after this, the family moved to a house in Summerhill. From all I have heard of Ann Grace, I realise she must have been a capable person with a strong sense of duty, and I imagine she would take on the task of

[5] See Preface.

29

finding suitable foster-parents for her two very young nieces.

There were two daughters at the house in Summerhill, high up above the town, near the then new church of St. Seiriol. In this same church, during the first World War, I often saw an elderly member of the congregation — a Miss Johnstone — and recently learned that she was the daughter of one of the girls at the house in Summerhill.

This house had a garden with an orchard, and long afterwards, Grace recalled the storing of many apples in one of the attics and even on top of the large fourposter beds, and that she and Ann were sometimes tempted to help themselves to an apple after they had been put to bed. The girls seem to have been happy, well trained in housewifely arts, and attending the National School where their aunt had been appointed. Headmistress in 1856.

Of the two older girls we know that Mary, a lively, high-spirited girl, evidently found Aunt Ann's regime too repressive, for at sixteen she ran away from home and later married a French mariner named Gibeaud. Little was heard of her for many years. Margaret remained in Holyhead and married John William Gannon. Ann, the youngest daughter of William Hughes married John Thomas Hawley in March 1884. Their younger daughter known to us as Cousin Annie is a lively and alert eighty-four, and was until recently an active member of the Llanfawr Women's Institute of which she was a founder member.[6]

When Grace Hughes was about fifteen years old, she became under-nursemaid to the children of Captain Charles B. C. Dent, R.N. Before coming to Holyhead where he was to be Marine Superintendent for twenty-six years, Captain Dent had had a distinguished naval career. His wife was the eldest daughter of Sir Demetrius Courcumelli, of Corfu.[7] With this family, Grace received the training which later made her such a splendid mother to her own large family of

[6] Cousin Annie died on May 24th, 1972.
[7] " The Times ", 21st March, 1894 — Obituary Notice.

nine. When Grace was nearly twenty, and now senior nursemaid, the Dents were to spend some time in Italy, and very much wanted Grace to accompany them. Her father was away at sea; her foster-parents could not give their consent to the plan, and also Grace had now met the man she was to marry later that year, and perhaps she, too, was reluctant to leave Holyhead, although happy with the Dents and very fond of her small charges.

Grace married Clifford James Wyndham Ballyn on July 17th, 1872, at St. Cybi's Church, Holyhead. This was the bridegroom's twenty-sixth birthday, Grace being twenty.

Grace Hughes, now Grace Ballyn evidently remained in close touch with the Dents for some years after their return to Holyhead. The Dents settled in a large house* at the top of Thomas Street, and before moving to a house in Church Terrace, the young Ballyns lived in a much smaller house, lower down, 15 Thomas Street. The christenings of young Dents and young Ballyns appear almost alternately in the registers of St. Cybi's Church, Mrs. Dent and Grace having the usual Victorian large families. Mrs. Dent gave Grace a beautiful pelisse for her first child's christening — and a pretty mahogany cot which is still in the family.

The accompanying photograph shows Grace as a young married woman of twenty-one with her first child, Richard. The dress she wears had been her wedding dress, and I am told it was made of heavy corded cream silk. The bodice is close fitting and trimmed with fringe of a darker colour. She has a very Welsh face with delicate features and dark deep-set eyes. My father used to tell me that his mother had very dark hair and beautiful colouring. Her face is sensitive and gentle. I can see in this face the kindness and affection which made me so happy as her grandchild, nearly forty years later.

Before beginning to follow this climb up the family tree of Grace Hughes, the reader may care to see with what authentic facts the search was begun, and these are therefore set out below.

* Garreg Domas.

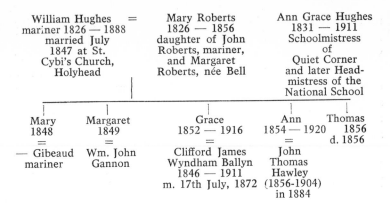

William Hughes =	Mary Roberts	Ann Grace Hughes
mariner 1826 — 1888	1826 — 1856	1831 — 1911
married July	daughter of John	Schoolmistress
1847 at St.	Roberts, mariner,	of
Cybi's Church,	and Margaret	Quiet Corner
Holyhead	Roberts, née Bell	and later Head-
		mistress of the
		National School

Mary	Margaret	Grace	Ann	Thomas
1848	1849	1852 — 1916	1854 — 1920	1856
=	=	=	=	d. 1856
— Gibeaud	Wm. John	Clifford James	John	
mariner	Gannon	Wyndham Ballyn	Thomas	
		1846 — 1911	Hawley	
		m. 17th July, 1872	(1856-1904)	
			in 1884	

And so on my main stem the name Hughes disappeared, but I still had innumerable cousins who must still bear the name and for these I continued to search.

Holyhead harbour from St. Cybi's Churchyard

(from a print of about 1830)

Grace Ballyn, aged 21, with her first child, Richard James.

CHAPTER 4

The Grandparents of Grace Hughes and the entrance of H.H.H. into the story

I WAS now in completely unknown territory, for Do's knowledge of her grandfather's generation did not extend beyond the vague memory of her grandfather, William, the mariner, and Aunt Ann Grace whom, of course, she remembered very well indeed. Among the collection of photographs in what I call her 'Welsh box' are some very handsome Welsh faces, but alas! she is unable to identify more than one or two of these. My grandmother was virtually an orphan from the age of five and so missed the usual stories handed down from mother to daughter. The facts which have been recorded are all of distant cousins in collateral branches. However, these have proved most valuable in extending the branches of the family tree far and wide.

On two points, however, Do was insistent. According to her, we were connected with the farm, Ty Mawr Mynydd, and with Hugh Hugh Hughes, the benefactor of whom more later.

Meanwhile, my aim was to climb, so I began to look for the parents of William, the mariner.

They proved to be Thomas and Grace Hughes and Thomas was a gardener. Their eldest son, Thomas, was baptized on Christmas Day 1823. I found the baptism of William was on October 4th, 1829, together with that of a brother, Charles.[8] Were these twins? Later, of course, I found from William's marriage certificate that he had been born in 1826, so this

---

[*] St. Cybi's Church Registers.

was a late baptism. Thomas and Grace were somewhat care-
less about the christening of their children, for at this point
I found no record of the christening of Ann Grace whom I
knew must have been born in 1830 or 1831. Much later on
I found her baptism, a very late one indeed: " Ann, an adult
aged 23, daughter of Thomas and Grace Hughes, Mill
Street ", and with this was the baptism of a younger sister,
" Catherine, an adult aged 18, daughter of Thomas and
Grace Hughes of Mill Street ". The date was 1st July. 1853.[9]

Do had never heard of Catherine, though she may well
have been named after her. I have sometimes wondered if
there were any other daughters of whose existence I have
no knowledge. After more experience of these searches I
realised that parents often never troubled to have daughters
christened, but only the sons.

The parents of these five children had been married at
St. Cybi's Church on November 25th, 1822, the bride's name
being Grace Hill.[10] The name Hill appears from time to time
in the St. Cybi's Church Registers, the earliest one being a
record of baptism of Jane, daughter of Anthony and Delilah
Hill on January 23rd, 1704. There is another baptism record
in 1714 of twin daughters of Anthony and Delilah and he is
described as ' Irishman '. I later discovered a Rent Roll of the
Presaddfed and the Penrhos Estate drawn up by a Captain
Hill and dated February 12th, 1689.[11]

It was some months later that I learned that the eldest
son, Thomas, born in 1823 eventually became a Customs
Official at Liverpool. There are several references to him in
family letters, the latest one being in a letter dated 13th
November, 1863, where he is described as being " in the
3 class out of door officer ". Of Charles, the third son, I have
discovered nothing more, but the entry in the St. Cybi's
Burial Registers, — " Charles Hughes, September 1843 aged
fourteen " must refer to him. The name Charles was not in
common use in Holyhead at that time, except in my own
family.

[9] St. Cybi's Registers. [10] St. Cybi's Registers. [11] Penrhos Papers VII 497

The subsequent history of Ann Grace is well known in the family. She spent some months teaching in London in 1853 and part of 1854, but returned to Holyhead as she was very unwell. She refers to this in a letter dated April 24th, 1854, to her cousin, William Hughes, saying that her father had travelled to London to bring her home earlier that year. It is well known in the family that Ann had had an unhappy love affair, being jilted by a curate to whom she had become engaged. Perhaps this unhappy incident was the cause of her long illness, for she was home for some weeks, before returning to London for a period of six months at the end of which time she was to take an examination. She was appointed Headmistress of the National School in 1856. It is not known how long she remained here, nor the exact period during which she had her private school, but we do know from Census Returns that by 1861 she was living at No. 8, Swift Square. She was a good churchwoman all her life, attending St. Cybi's Church, not only on Sundays but every Friday for Welsh Evensong. However, as soon as the officiating clergyman went into the pulpit to deliver his sermon, she rose and left the church. Was this to show disapproval of the treatment meted out to her by the curate who had jilted her? Do tells me that, on many occasions she saw her rise with great dignity and leave the church. In no other way was she eccentric. In late life she developed a slightly shuffling walk, and old Nina Ballyn rather unkindly referred to her as " Aunt Ann, double shuffle ". On retirement, Ann Grace went to live in rooms in Alderley Terrace, near St. Seiriol's Church, receiving an annuity from the Hugh Hughes Charity. The scheme for the administration of the money which had been provided under the will of Hugh Hugh Hughes, signed in 1887 was finally put into operation in 1893. At this time Ann Grace would be over sixty and was reputed to be comfortably off. She died intestate in 1911, and her second niece, Margaret Gannon, was granted letters of administration. The runaway niece, Mary, was after some difficulty traced and found to be in Liverpool, a widow living in a home for the dependants of mariners. The little estate was divided among the four nieces, each niece receiving ninety pounds. By today's values, three hundred and sixty pounds would be about three thousand pounds which seems a large sum for a poor schoolmistress to have amassed. I was later to discover that she had been remembered in the will of more than one of her cousins. Her death had been registered by W. Jones, nephew, of King's Road. Was he the son of Aunt Ann's sister, Catherine, or a more distant relative called . . . in Welsh fashion nephew, and why did he not receive a share of the money? There was a story current in the famiy, that a certain William Jones, kinsman of Aunt Ann's visited her frequently, but no one could give me his exact relationship to us.

About this time in the search, I had learned from Do that Hugh Hugh Hughes who had founded the Hugh Hughes Charity had been her mother's uncle. I have already mentioned the almost Elizabethan method of referring to kinsmen which obtains among the Welsh. So far there had been no kinsman of this name found during the search, and no one in the family seemed to know exactly how we were related.

I learned a good deal more about the Charity from the Rev. Canon D. T. Davies who, interested in our supposed relationship to Hugh Hugh Hughes, gave me a copy of the " Scheme for the regulation and management of the Charity founded by Hugh Hugh Hughes by his will dated 10th December, 1887 ". I sent to Somerset House for a copy of his death certificate and of his will, hoping the latter would provide some clue to our relationship. The will showed him to have been a wealthy and generous man leaving a life interest in property, and annuities for many of his relatives. No one of our branch of the family was mentioned, unless one of the widows who had received legacies should prove to be the link. Ten thousand pounds had been left " for the maintenance or relief of poor or necessitous persons either male or female, and without reference to their religious belief or creed, resident in the parish of Holyhead, in the County of Anglesey ". I now resolved to try to climb a little higher up the family tree, hoping to find the connection with Hugh, while doing so. It was really the main stem of the tree in which I was interested.

So far my task had been fairly straightforward, but now real difficulties began. Looking back, I can find various reason for this, not least of all my own inexperience and impulsiveness in jumping to conclusions on insufficient evidence. The Welsh surnames and the endless repetition of a very limited number of Christian names added to the general confusion. As one goes farther back in time, there is less detailed information in the parish registers. Some of the family myths led me up paths which seemed to be cul-de-sacs. One of these in particular, led me far away from my main stem, but as Do and Cousin Annie were very positive that " the Hughes's of Ty Mawr Mynydd belonged to us ", I spent a good deal of time investigating their claims without success. I returned to Thomas, the gardener and began to search for his baptism.

It seems wise at this point to insert a copy of the pedigree before we become completely bogged down with the various people nearly all named William Hughes, Hugh Hughes or Catherine Hughes.

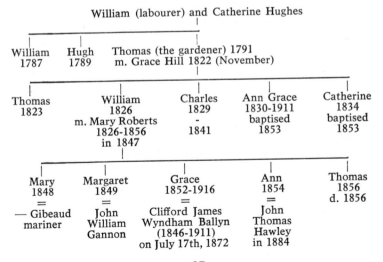

William (labourer) and Catherine Hughes

William 1787	Hugh 1789	Thomas (the gardener) 1791 m. Grace Hill 1822 (November)		
Thomas 1823	William 1826 m. Mary Roberts 1826-1856 in 1847	Charles 1829 - 1841	Ann Grace 1830-1911 baptised 1853	Catherine 1834 baptised 1853
Mary 1848 = — Gibeaud mariner	Margaret 1849 = John William Gannon	Grace 1852-1916 = Clifford James Wyndham Ballyn (1846-1911) on July 17th, 1872	Ann 1854 = John Thomas Hawley in 1884	Thomas 1856 d. 1856

37

The first William on this little pedigree proved to be the father of Thomas. Thomas was baptised on April 3rd, 1791, son of William, labourer, and Catherine. There were two older sons, William baptised on September 30th, 1787, and Hugh on January 25th, 1789.[12] No other children of William, labourer and Catherine — a very small family for those days. I also failed to find any record of the marriage of these parents. I began to search through the neighbouring parishes and while I was waiting for replies from the National Library of Wales, turned my attention to Hugh, second son of William and Catherine. Perhaps he was the grandfather of Hugh Hugh Hughes. This surmise is not as fanciful as it may sound, for at this early date there was at least one advantage. In 1800 there were not more than two thousand people in the parish of Holyhead and entries in the St. Cybi registers were fewer. By this time, my friend, John Bulmer, had lent me one of the copies of the Holyhead registers which he had made some years previously, so that I could always consult this whenever I " had a hunch " about a problem. I'm afraid the Hughes's were constantly with me, when I was washing up, gardening, walking or embroidering! A Hugh Hughes married Jane Jones, widow, in 1813. His eldest child was christened Robert, in 1814. I then sent to Somerset House for the birth certificate of Hugh Hugh Hughes born in 1844, according to the age given on his death certificate. He was now shown to be the son of Robert Hughes, engineer of Market Street, Holyhead. A second son, Richard Edward, was born in 1847, and the family were then living in Boston Street. A search was then made for the marriage certificate of Robert Hughes, engineer of Holyhead. He had married Elizabeth Lewis, daughter of Richard Lewis, mariner. His father's name was stated to be Hugh Hughes, labourer, so I thought the founder of the Charity could be a second cousin to my grandmother, Grace Hughes, and called in Welsh fashion, ' uncle '.

[12] St. Cybi's Parish Registers.

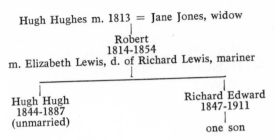

Hugh Hughes m. 1813 = Jane Jones, widow

Robert
1814-1854
m. Elizabeth Lewis, d. of Richard Lewis, mariner

Hugh Hugh
1844-1887
(unmarried)

Richard Edward
1847-1911

one son

This descent of Hugh Hugh Hughes, who founded the Hugh Hugh Hughes Charity is accurate, but I was soon to find that his grandfather, Hugh Hughes, was not the second son of William and Catherine.

While waiting for the result of the search for the marriage of William and Catherine, I looked for William's baptism, working backwards from 1765. At that time there were about three hundred families in the parish, and the population was about twelve hundred. Baptisms averaged forty-two each year and in 1761 I found the baptism of William, son of William and Margaret Hughes on January 18th and another William, son of William and Catherine Hughes, baptised on June 11th. One of these was undoubtedly my forebear, but which one?

Do had repeatedly stressed that her mother was connected with the family at Ty Mawr Mynydd. This is an old farm situated on the lower slopes of Holyhead Mountain, hence the word 'mynydd' following the name, Ty Mawr. It was on the land of this farm that the famous Stone Age Hut Circles were found. I now began again to investigate from this angle.

The parish registers showed the baptisms of eight children born to Hugh and Mary Hughes, of Ty Mawr Mynydd between 1815 and 1835. The family appears in the Census Returns for 1841 and 1851 at Ty Mawr Mynydd. Hugh is shown to have been born at Holyhead, and Mary at Llanfihangel, Anglesey. Their marriage appears in the Llanfihangel-yn-Howyn Bishop's Transcripts for 1814, October 18th, — Hugh Hughes of Holyhead, by licence, to Mary Williams of this parish.[13] At the time of the 1861 Census Returns, Hugh is still at Ty Mawr, a widower, aged seventy-two. An unmarried daughter, Mary, is still living at home. This might be the Miss Hughes of Ty Mawr Mynydd of whom I had so often heard. According to the three Census Returns Hugh had been born in 1789. Now the only Hugh Hughes baptised in that year was mine — the second son of my William and Catherine — and yet I could not really decide that Hugh at Ty Mawr Mynydd and my Hugh were one and the same person. I next wrote to Somerset House asking for a search to be made for the will of Hugh Hughes, Ty Mawr Mynydd aged 80, whose death, in December 1869, I had by now discovered.

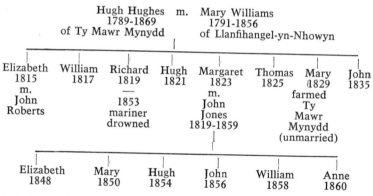

All these facts came from the St. Cybi registers (except Hugh's marriage) or from Census Returns. Did this Hugh of Ty Mawr Mynydd belong to my tree? Was he the elder brother of Thomas the gardener? If so, he could not be the grandfather of the Hugh who founded the Charity and who was also firmly planted in the family legend.

In due course, a copy of the will of Hugh Hughes, Ty Mawr Mynydd, arrived. The estate, according to probate was valued at three thousand pounds. Each living son and daughter had been remembered equally. After the deaths of

[13] Found for me by John Bulmer.

40

the two married daughters and the one surviving son-in-law, money and property was to be divided equally among his six grandchildren. Mary, the unmarried daughter was the residuary legatee and at her death, the grandchildren would inherit her estate. The widowed daughter is described as Margaret Jones, and her husband, John Jones as "late Light-keeper of South Stack Lighthouse." Mary is appointed sole executrix and three trustees are named — Chancellor Briscoe (the Vicar), William Jones, Bodwina, and Lewis Jones, Llwyn Onn, both nephews of the deceased.

Some of these facts could fit into the stories I had heard. Mary, the unmarried daughter could be "the Miss Hughes of Ty Mawr Mynydd", and the child, William Jones, born 1858, could be the "nephew" of Ann Grace Hughes who had registered her death in 1911. But who were the nephews, William and Lewis Jones? As far as I had yet discovered, Hugh Hughes had no sister who had married a Jones. I did not really feel I had conclusive proof that the Ty Mawr Mynydd people were a collateral branch of my family. I should like to trace the relationship if only because of the strong tradition that there was in this link, but my main interest, of course, was to climb as high as I could up the tree. I now had Thomas, the gardener as my authentic fore-bear whose elder brother, Hugh, might be of Ty Mawr Mynydd or Hugh Hughes, grandfather of the founder of the Hugh Hughes Charity.

CHAPTER 5

Two more families are added as Collateral Branches

THESE two possible collateral branches were put on one side for the moment, and I returned to the pursuit of William and Catherine, waiting for an answer from the National Library of Wales, about their marriage. I hoped to find it in one of the parishes adjacent to Holyhead.

I now seemed to be facing an insoluble problem. Was the present head of my pedigree William, son of William and Margaret Hughes, baptised on January 18th, 1761, or William, son of William and Catherine Hughes, baptised on June 11th, 1761? There were no other possible candidates for my William's parents. I had also spent much time in following side tracks which had apparently led me nowhere. However, I was to find later, that all this work had not been time wasted. What I most wanted now was news of the marriage of William and Catherine.

It was the remembering of a casual remark made by my father, over forty years previously, that sent me off on the path that was to lead to the solving of more than one problem. We were at that time living in Valley, three miles from Holyhead, and my father was home from sea. Finding I had a new friend, Enid Owen, Penmynydd, near the village of Caergeiliog, near Valley, my father one day told me that he was related to Enid's mother, through his own mother, once Grace Hughes. At the time, this information fell on heedless ears — I accepted what was said but did not ask my father to explain the exact relationship, and soon forgot what I had been told. Now I suddenly remembered the incident and bitterly regretted my casual response. If I could trace the relationship, would it help me in my search? It might at any rate provide me with another collateral branch to the pedigree.

Enid was now dead, but her first cousin, Trevor Lloyd of Ty Mawr, Holyhead, might be able to help me. I knew that Enid and Trevor's mothers were sisters, so he too, could be related to us. I had met Trevor once, many years previously, and on the strength of that I got in touch with him. This meeting proved both pleasant and rewarding. Trevor knew my sister and had known two of my brothers, and this was another link. He also proved to be a very old friend of John Bulmer's. Trevor had a pedigree which had been worked out by John, from the St. Cybi's Parish registers and from information supplied by Trevor.

This pedigree went back through Lloyds and Jones's to a William and Catherine Hughes whose marriage had not been traced. They had had three daughters, only one of whom survived. This was Elizabeth, Trevor's great-grandmother, born in 1795. Her father, William Hughes of Ty'n Pwll, had been Land Steward to Sir John Stanley of Penrhos. William, according to the parish registers died in September 1820, aged fifty-nine. He must have been born in 1761 . . . was he the son of William and Margaret, or of William and Catherine?

I made a copy of Trevor's pedigree, promising to let him know what I discovered. On my return home, I looked for a possible link between us, finally setting out the two pedigrees side by side, and this is what I saw in the first two generations —

William Hughes and Catherine			William Hughes and Catherine		
labourer			farmer of Ty'n Pwll	d. 1799	
born 1761			1761-1820		
No record of the marriage			No record of the marriage		
William	Hugh	Thomas	Elizabeth	Catherine	Catherine
1787	1789	1791	1795	1797	1799
		(the gardener,	Trevor's	d.	d.
		my great-great	great-	infant	infant
		grandfather	grandmother)		

It was very tempting to conclude that these two sets of parents were really the one couple and that the six children were brothers and sisters. And also, if I assumed Hugh, born in 1789 to be Hugh of Ty Mawr Mynydd, I should at one fell swoop not only have established the link between Trevor, Enid and my own branch, but settled once and for all the elusive cousins from Ty Mawr Mynydd.

However, I was hesitant to accept this. It seemed almost too good to be true. There was absolutely no tradition in my family of any link with a farm called Ty'n Pwll, nor of a forebear who had been Land Steward to Sir John Stanley. Ty'n Pwll had been demolished in the early 1840's, as it lay in the path of the proposed new railway. Elizabeth and her husband, William Jones, who had succeeded Elizabeth's father at Ty'n Pwll had moved into the new house built to replace Ty'n Pwll. This was the Ty Mawr which eventually became Trevor's home. William Jones, son-in-law of William Hughes, farmed the land of Ty Mawr and of Ty'n Pwll, for in 1841 he appears in the list of those paying tithes, and in 1867 his son, Owen Jones, appears in the list of Penrhos rentals as paying rent on Ty Mawr and Ty'n Pwll. The farm Ty Mawr lies on the Ty'n Pwll Road. Why was none of this current in the family stories; I suppose my father could have told me most of this if only I had shown any interest in his remark.

The fact that the father of William, Hugh and Thomas was described as a labourer, and the father of Elizabeth and the two Catherines as a farmer, also made me doubt if they were all one family. I should have realised that in Holy Island at that time, the term labourer usually meant farm labourer — very often the son of a farmer perhaps working on his father's farm until he married and acquired a farm of his own.

About a month later I was in Holyhead again and this time a very careful scrutiny of the St. Cybi registers themselves revealed the following in the Baptism Register —

44

Sept. 30th, 1787, William, son of William, labourer and Catherine

Jan. 25th, 1789, Hugh, son of William, labourer and Catherine.

April 3rd, 1791, Thomas, son of William, labourer and Catherine.

April 2, 1793, James and Richard, sons of William, farmer and Catherine.

June 14th, 1795, Elizabeth, daughter of William, farmer and Catherine.

Feb. 4th, 1797, Catherine, daughter of William, farmer and Catherine.

June 26th, 1799, Catherine, daughter of William, farmer and Catherine.

This looked more than ever like one family, but how strange that the twins had been overlooked in both pedigrees.

Yes! These people *must* all belong to me. I did what I should have done a month previously — wrote to the Keeper of the Records at the National Library of Wales to see if they had the will of William Hughes, Ty'n Pwll, who died in 1820, and waited hopefully for a favourable reply.

When I reached home, there was a letter from John Bulmer awaiting me, giving me the date of the missing marriage of William and Catherine. He had found this in his transcription of the Llanfaethlu registers. Llanfaethlu is a village about ten miles from Holyhead on the larger island of Anglesey.

The entry in the Marriage Register was as follows — *14th July, 1786,* William Hughes of Holyhead, bachelor, and Catherine Williams of Llanfaethlu, spinster. Witnesses: Richard Williams and William Hughes. The witnesses were probably fathers of the newly-married couple.

I had told John of my recent discoveries in the Holyhead registers and he had himself wondered if William of Ty'n Pwll was the common ancestor of Trevor and myself. He knew too, why I was doubtful about this. I now firmly claimed this marriage to be that of the parents of William, Hugh and Thomas, the date being just right.

Within a week or two a xerox copy of the will of William Hughes, Ty'n Pwll, arrived. It was dated June 18th, 1813.

Three dwelling houses with courts, yards and other appurtenances were left to his wife, Elin, and at her death these were to go to his daughter, Elizabeth. His wife was also to receive the interest from certain money, and one feather bed, bedstead and best bedding as her own goods and chattels for ever. His daughter, Elizabeth, is left a house, and other property is left " unto and for the use of my son, Thomas Hughes, his heirs, executors and assigns . . . but upon this special trust and confidence that my said son Thomas Hughes shall and do pay out of the rents and profits of the said premises unto my sons William Hughes, James Hughes and Richard Hughes the sum of Two pounds annually " . . . " I give and bequeath to my natural daughter, Mary Hughes by Catherine Hughes the sum of Ten pounds to be paid to her at the end of six months. The residue and remainder of my goods chattels effects and personal estate whatsoever I give and bequeath the same unto and amongst my said children Elizabeth Hughes, William Hughes, Hugh Hughes, Thomas Hughes, James Hughes and Richard Hughes to be equally divided ".

The signature is firm and clear but that on the codicil which is dated July 27th, 1820, is very shaky. This was a few days before his death, the entry in the Burials register being dated August 5th, 1820. In the codicil he leaves his wife, Elin, a further five pounds, and confirms and ratifies in all particulars his will signed in 1813.

So here was the evidence I needed, and I was delighted to have taken another step up the family tree. I was, of course, annoyed with myself for refusing to accept what now seemed only too obvious.

William's second marriage was found in the St. Cybi registers — William Hughes, widower, to Ellin Zabulon, widow. 2nd October, 1809. His natural daughter was born during his widowerhood. Her baptism is in the St. Cybi registers — May 28th, 1808, Mary, illegitimate daughter of William Hughes, farmer and Catherine Hughes both of this parish. I am glad that her father remembered her in his will.

When next I went to visit Do, I took William Hughes's will, wishing to show it to Trevor, so that he might see proof of our relationship, and take notes of anything he might wish to add to his own tree. I also put among my papers the will of Hugh, Ty Mawr Mynydd, as I thought Trevor might possibly recognise names of one or two of the legatees as one of the vague Welsh " uncles " or " aunts ", and perhaps help me to clear up the mystery of another of the family stories.

Both Do, and Trevor, when he called to see us, seemed quite fascinated by the will of William Hughes and all it revealed. I told them I hoped to discover more about William's eldest son, William, and also the twins, James and Richard.

We then turned to the will of Hugh Hughes, Ty Mawr Mynydd (see page 40). Do had already seen it and was convinced that Hugh's grandson, William Jones, born in 1858 was the " nephew " who had registered the death of Ann Grace Hughes in 1911. She was also certain that Mary Hughes, born in 1829, the daughter who remained at Ty Mawr Mynydd after her father's death was the Miss Hughes about whom she had heard her mother talk when, she, Do was a child.

When Do mentioned William Jones, supposed nephew of Ann Grace Hughes, she described him in detail, and said he had lived in King's Road. " Of course! I remember him well," said Trevor. " He had a beard, and I remember his three daughters — they were cousins of ours. They lived in Craig-y-don when I knew them." Well this was a very promising beginning. Trevor picked up the will again and when he read the names of two of the trustees, William Jones Bodwina, and Lewis Jones, Llwynn Onn, he exclaimed, " Well! These two nephews of Hugh are my great-grandmother's eldest sons — Elizabeth Jones's sons! Lewis became estate agent to the Marquess of Anglesey."

And so I had another collateral branch to add to the pedigree and Do was well satisfied that another of her stories of the past had proved to be true. The family from Ty Mawr Mynydd were now firmly added to the pedigree; my father's remark so many years before had led to the search for our relationship with Enid Owen, and with Trevor Lloyd and this was established. William and Catherine of Ty'n Pwll were our ancestors.

The next step was to discover whether William Hughes of Ty'n Pwll had been baptised son of William and Margaret in January 1761, or son of William and Catherine in June 1761.

I also very much wished to meet my distant cousin who had descended from Hugh Hughes, Ty Mawr Mynydd. It is a pity that about two months elapsed before the second wish came true, for it would have saved me a good deal of trouble in my efforts to clear up the first mystery.

However, while waiting to meet my newly-found cousin, I began to tackle this mystery of the parentage of William Hughes, Ty'n Pwll.

Clifford James Wyndham Ballyn in 1870 aged 24.

Holyhead Market Place in 1786.

CHAPTER 6

Three farmers all named William Hughes now cause
confusion, but a will points to ours

Now followed a search in the Holyhead Registers for the
families of William and Margaret, and William and
Catherine. The first William was baptised in 1732, son of
David and Jane Hughes. In November 1752 he married
Margaret Davies. They had five children, the first daughter,
Jane, born in 1753 evidently died young, for the second
daughter baptised in 1758 was also named Jane. The eldest
son was Hugh, born in 1755, my possible William, baptised
in January 1761 and the last child, David, baptised in 1762,
his mother, Margaret, dying at his birth. William himself
died in 1774 and is described as William Hughes, widower
of Ty Mawr, in the burial register.

This Ty Mawr was one of four farms on Holy Island, all
bearing the same name! This one lay on the west side of the
island, not far from Porthdafarch, and was adjacent to the
farm Mynydd Gof Du which had been farmed by William's
father, David Hughes and William's elder brother, David.
William Hughes, 1732-1774 was succeeded at this remote
Ty Mawr by his son, Hugh, who remained there till his death
in 1824, and was succeeded by another David, perhaps his
son.[14] The son, William, I had to ignore for the time being,
until I had a look at the other family. But I must admit I
had no feeling of kinship with this family. I worked backwards on their pedigree and in the St. Cybi Registers it went
back very plainly and easily to one Evan Hughes whose

[14] Penrhos Papers II, 775.

first son, William, had been buried in 1697. William 1732-1774 had descended from another son, David, christened in August 1696 and married to Jane Roberts in June 1722.

The second William had married Catherine Davies on the 23rd February, 1759 and their children were Elizabeth, February 20th, 1760; William, June 11th, 1761; Richard, July 30th, 1763 (may have died September 1763); Thomas, August 24th, 1764 and Hugh, December 6th, 1767. The father of those children is described as a farmer. I could not find a baptism date which seemed authentic for him and so could not trace his parents.[15]

A lease was granted in 1768 by Sir John Thomas Stanley, for sixty years to a William Hughes for Llys-y-gwynt, a farm of thirteen acres " in addition to the property of Ty Mawr late in the possession of Huw Morris and now of the said William Hughes ".[16] The lease among other clauses ensures that William would do " four days' reaping at Harvest time and two days' carriage with a team drawn by horses or oxen of Turffs or Sods yearly." I deliberately include the name ' Huw Morris ', as this name was to appear again, before much time elapsed. The Ty Mawr mentioned in this lease was later called Yr Efail Bach,[17] a smallholding of six acres. The word ' Efail ' means smithy. It was quite near Llys-y-gwynt and facing the coach road, may have offered services to a carriage horse in need of shoeing, or even have done repairs to a vehicle in distress on the rough roads of those days. At the beginning of the 19th century Thomas Telford was surveying the whole of the road from London to Holyhead. A contemporary of his describes the Anglesey road as " a miserable tract, composed of a succession of circuitous and craggy inequalities." The Anglesey Turnpike Trust was responsible for the road across the county, but in a sparsely populated area, with few tolls from the moderate traffic, keeping the road in good repair was quite beyond their powers. So we can see that help to travellers from ' Yr Efail

[15] St. Cybi's Parish Registers.
[16] Penrhos Papers III, 28.
[17] Penrhos Papers II, 775.

Bach' would be welcome. The farmhouse is still there and the name on its gate is 'Refail Bach'. Today, of course, the road we now know as the A5 is a few yards from the farm — but on the side of the road is now a garage, not a smithy. Surprisingly, few people seem to know that this road is Telford's road — but I am glad that he is remembered in the name of a new town on the A5 — Telford, in Shropshire.

A further search of the Parish Burial Registers added more confusion to the problem for I found a farmer, William Hughes, had died in April 1793 and another farmer, William Hughes, had died in June 1810. One of these must be William of Llys-y-gwynt, and the other could be William, son of the delicate William and Margaret of Ty Mawr who had died at an early age. Both were described as 'farmers'.

William who died in 1793 had rented "two quillets in Llanfair Bach and one quillet in Ty'n Pwll" and his widow did the same for the following two years.[18] The quillet in Ty'n Pwll was then added to the farm land at Ty'n Pwll itself, now rented by William Hughes, the Land Steward. There were at least two of the same name who had very small holdings of one or two acres.

A request to the National Library at Aberystwyth for the copies of the wills of the three William's produced those of William, Ty Mawr, who had died in 1774 and of William, Llys-y-gwynt, who had died in 1810. There was no will of the third William of Llanfair Bach. But later, I learned that he was an early kinsman of Trevor's, grandfather of William Jones, and sub-land agent to the Owens of Penrhos.

After reading the wills I was convinced that William of Llys-y-gwynt was the father of William Hughes, Ty'n Pwll. All the sons were named in order of dates of baptism. Varying sums of money were left and cattle and farm equipment was shared among them. His wife, Catherine, was the residuary legatee. The estate was valued at under £100. The names which appeared again in the Ty'n Pwll family and the close proximity of the two families, for at that time Ty'n Pwll

[18] Penrhos Rentals 1792, 1793, 1794.

and Llys-y-gwynt were less than half a mile apart, made me feel certain that William of Llys-y-gwynt now headed the pedigree. Less than a month later I was proved to be right! One other tiny piece of evidence, also seemed to point to a connection between William, Llys-y-gwynt and his son at Ty'n Pwll. Both men appear in the list of Churchwardens, at intervals during the late eighteenth and early nineteenth centuries.

While this part of the search continued, Trevor had undertaken to get in touch with his cousin, Freda Beck Jones, one of the direct descendants of Hugh Hughes, Ty Mawr Mynydd. He had always known she was a cousin because his mother had spoken of the family as cousins and he now told me that Freda was the second daughter of William Jones, whom Trevor and I now knew to be a grandson of Hugh Hughes, Ty Mawr Mynydd.

On my next visit to Holyhead, Trevor was asked what progress he had made. " Well, I rang Freda, and asked her many questions about her father, and her descent from Ty Mawr Mynydd. I explained that you wished to know all this."

" Well! Of course, I remember Hilda Ballyn very well indeed, but why is she so interested in my family? "

" Because she's your cousin," Trevor replied.

Freda was naturally quite astonished but very interested and helpful, giving Trevor her full pedigree back to Hugh Hughes, 1789-1869. Trevor gave me this, together with Freda's address. The pedigree corroborated what I had discovered, and added a good deal more new information. I wrote to thank Freda for all she had sent me, and received a very warm invitation to visit her, when I was next working at Bangor. This led to my spending a day at Menai Bridge with Freda and her husband. It was a case of friendship at first sight and each meeting since that day has been as pleasant as our first encounter.

To Freda I owe the first two names which I can now put above that of William Hughes, Llys-y-gwynt, for she not

April 6th 1834

Morris Jones from Llanddwfnan
was the father of Hugh Morris
Refal Bach, and Hugh Morris
Refal Bach was the father of
William Hughes Llys y gwynt.
William Hughes Llys y gwynt
was the father of William Hughs
Tyn y Pwll, William Hughes
Tyn y Pwll was the father
Hugh Hughes Ty Mawr Near
South Stack Holyhead is the
father of Eliz:th Hughes & Willi-
am, Richard, Hugh and
Margaret, Thomas and
Mary, and John.

Fascimile of Entry in the Tŷ Mawr Mynydd Family Bible
dated April 6th, 1834.

only let me make a copy of all the entries in her great-grand-father's family Bible, — information which corroborated all I had found in the Parish Registers — but gave me the following note, written by Hugh Hughes, Ty Mawr Mynydd, on April 6th, 1834.

"Morris Jones from Llanddyfnan was the father of Hugh Morris, Refail Bach, and Hugh Morris, Refail Bach, was the father of William Hughes, Llys-y-gwynt. William Hughes, Llys-y-gwynt, was the father of William Hughes, Ty'n Pwll. William Hughes, Ty'n Pwll, was the father of Hugh Hughes, Ty Mawr, near South Stack, Holyhead. Hugh Hughes is the father of Elizabeth Hughes and William, Richard, Hugh and Margaret, Thomas and Mary and John."

So here were two more generations handed to me as a gift, undoubtedly authentic and taking us back to the time when Morris Jones's son would be Hugh ap Morris and his son would be William ap Hugh who became William Hughes for by the end of the 17th century and the beginning of the 18th century the change over to surnames was gradually taking place.

Quite recently, I learned from my youngest brother that the Chinese still follow the old Welsh custom, so that on paper, one cannot see any visible relationship between a man and his grandson.

It was now very easy to realise why I had failed to find a father for William of Llys-y-gwynt, because I had expected his father to have the surname Hughes.* This fresh information also settled once and for all which of the Williams baptised in 1761 belonged to us. I knew too, where to look for Hugh Morris, — at Yr Efail Bach.

Hugh Hughes of Ty Mawr Mynydd would be twenty-one when his grandfather, William of Llys-y-gwynt, died and he may even have learned his pedigree from him.

If only I had met Freda earlier! How much easier my task would have been! However, it had been an absorbing hunt and a fresh trail had been cleared, for the next steps.

---

* See page 50. "I could not find a baptism date which seemed authentic for him and so could not trace his parents."

CHAPTER 7

The record in a Family Bible proves to be true

INFORMATION, or perhaps I should call it 'a little corroborative detail' about Hugh Morris and Morris Jones was scanty, but enough to prove they were real persons ond were linked to us.

Many of the entries in the early Parish Registers are illegible, — sometimes a surname is obliterated, sometimes a Christian name. There are also gaps on several of the early pages.

However, I did find certain baptisms in the Bishop's Transcripts of the St. Cybi Registers — July 17th, 1698, John, son of Maurice Jones; 1700, Owen, son of Maurice Jones; 1702, Jonet. In the burial register I found 21st February, 1697, Margaret, infant daughter of Maurice Jones. There are many gaps and undecipherable names in these early registers and I failed to find Hugh's name. There were probably sons named Richard and William, for these names together with that of Hugh, appear several times very closely linked in the Penrhos Lists for the next generation.

There is no record of a marriage of Morris Jones, but this may be one of the records now illegible or among those lost. Nor could I find his name in any of the earlier Penrhos Rental Lists. If we assume from the burial of his daughter, Margaret, in February, 1697, that she was the first child we may infer that he was married about 1695. There is also among the Penrhos Papers a lease dated June 24th, 1696,[19] which reads —

[19] Penrhos Papers VII, 136.

Be it remembered that it was then agreed between John Owen of Penrhos in ye County of Anglesey, Esq., of the one part, and Maurice Jones of Tre feibion Meurig in ye said County, miller, of the other part, as followeth:

First ye said John Owen doth demise and sett[20] unto ye said Maurice Jones, that salt water corn mill called Melin Heli lying in Holyhead in the sayd County, from the first day of August next for and during the term of two years at the rent of thirteen pounds every year, to be paid at each quarter of the said years by even and equal portions; that is to say, the sum of three pounds and five shillings quarterly during the sayd term; and also the sayd Maurice Jones grinding all the corn and grain which the said John Owen shall use in his house called Penrhos where he now dwelleth, toll free, and making his pilcorn;[21] the said Maurice Jones furnishing the said mill with cogs and rounds[22] from time to time as it shall be necessary; and the said John Owen is to allow the sayd Maurice Jones the keeping of one horse or mare during the said term. It is also agreed that ye sayd Maurice Jones shall surrender and yield up ye sayd mill unto the said John Owen at the end of ye first year if ye sayd Maurice Jones so pleaseth. In witness whereof ye sayd parties have interchangeably hereunto put their hands ye day and year above written.

Memo yt ye word three
was interlined before
ye signing hereof and then   The mark of
signed in ye presence of   Maurice Jones

William Griffith
Em. Griffith

It is not unreasonable to assume that the Maurice Jones named in this lease is our Maurice Jones, arrived in Holyhead

[20] Lease.
[21] Oats.
[22] Spindles.

Juney 24th, 696.

Be it remembered y'' it was then agreed Between
John Owen of Penrhos in y'' County of Anglesey Esq'' of
y'' one pte & Maurice Jones of An-fribin Mûing in y''
sayd Countie Miller of y'' other pte, as followeth:
First, y'' s'' Jo: Owen doth demise & sett unto y'' s'' Maurice
Jones y'' s'' watter Corn mill called Melin Heli
from y'' first day of August next for & during y'' term
of two years at y'' rent of thirteen pounds every year
to be payed at each qter of y'' sayd years by even & equall
porhions, y'' is to say y'' Sume of pounds & ffive shillings qterly during y'' s'' term; & also y'' s'' Maurice Jones
grinding all y'' Corn & graine w'' y'' s'' Jo: Owen shall use
in his Howse called Penrhos when hi now dwelleth toll-
free & makeing his pileven: the s'' Maurice Jones furnishing
y'' s'' Mill w'' Cogs & rounds from time to time as it shall
be necessary: & y'' s'' Jo: Owen is to allow y'' s'' Maurice Jones
y'' keeping of the this or more during y'' s'' term; It is also
agreed y'' y'' sayd Maurice Jones shall surrender & yeild
up y'' s'' Mill unto y'' s'' Jo: Owen at y'' end of y'' first year
if y'' sayd Maurice Jones soe pleaseth. In witness whereof
y'' s'' pties have hereunto put their hands y'' day & year above
written.

the mark of
Maurice (⬡) Jones.

memd y'' y'' word there was putt in
line above y'' Signing hereof &
then signed in y'' presence of

William Griffith. Em: Griffith

from Llanddyfnan by way of Tre feibion Meurig.[23] There is only one Maurice Jones (the name is sometimes spelt Morris) in the Parish Registers at this period — and the position of the mill is in the area where Maurice Jones's descendants lived for the next four or five generations. His great grandson, William Hughes 1761-1820 lived at Tre Gof, before moving to Ty'n Pwll. Tre Gof is a stone's throw from Felin Heli. Many gaps in the Burial Registers for probable years of the death of Morris Jones made the search for his death fruitless.

For the next generation more information was available. Hugh Morris and Richard Morris are co-tenants of Glany-Gors together with a Hugh Pritchard, in 1732. Each tenant pays £2.15.0 yearly to the landlord, Mr. William Owen of Penrhos and each provides two days' reaping annually and gifts of two capons.[24]

In 1730, on October 18th, Hugh Morris married Elin Jones, daughter of Owen and Anne Jones.[25] Several baptisms are missing for the months after this, and the first baptism we might accept is on the 16th April, 1735: William, son of . . . and Elin . . . Nearly all the Bishop's Transcripts for the following period up to November 1737, are missing, but on December 11th, 1737, we find Elizabeth, daughter of Hugh and Elin Morris; on 7th February, 1741, John, son of Hugh and Elin Morris; 20th March, 1745, Thomas. Hugh's name appears in the yearly Penrhos Rental Lists, now farming half of the Glan-y-Gors land, and giving service of three days' reaping and presents of capons annually.

At this time all the Penrhos tenants gave gifts and we find these vary from chickens, geese and capons to one dozen candles, one quart of honey, a bottle or bottles of brandy (smuggled?) and a quart of Usquebagh![*]

Much later we find Hugh Morris sharing the land of Glan-y-Gors with his son, William Hughes, who is also

[23] Today known as Treban Meurig.
[24] Penrhos Papers VII, 505
[25] St. Cybi's Parish Registers.
[*] Usquebagh — Whiskey.

renting the eleven acres of Llys-y-gwynt[26] for which William pays a rent of £5.10.0. The landlord is now Sir John Thomas Stanley who had married Margaret Owen, the heiress of Penrhos in 1763.

In 1757 Hugh is listed as one of the Churchwardens; in 1766 he was sharing the tenancy of Glan-y-Gors with his son, William, and living at Yr Efail Bach;[27] we realise that in 1768 he had been farming Yr Efail Bach for some years because of the reference to this in the lease given to William Hughes in September 1768 by Sir John Stanley.[28] Hugh died in 1768, being buried on January 22nd. This was the reason for the new lease granted to his son, William of Llys-y-gwynt who now farmed Yr Efail Bach (then called Ty Mawr and at that time adjoining Glan-y-Gors for Telford's road was not yet separating them) as well as Llys-y-gwynt, until his death in 1810.

From Hugh's will signed on 16th October, 1767, two new facts emerge. He had a second daughter, Elin, who does not appear in the Baptism Register. She was perhaps his first child whose name should fill one of the gaps in the Register. It would also appear from Hugh's will that he had lent his son, William, money at some earlier date, and the cancelling of this debt is referred to somewhat quaintly in the will.

" To my son, William I give and bequeath one pound in cash and my best coat also; and for all that my son William is indebted to me, I say I forgive them to him. Nobody is to ask him for them. Likewise I give and bequeath to my daughter Elin a bedstead and wainscoat chest marked with T.G. 1721. All the residue and remainder of my substance and effects whatsoever I do hereby bequeath to my dearly beloved wife and my daughter Elizabeth whom I appoint sole executors of this my Last Will and Testament."

It now seemed that I had finished my search and could reach no father backwards in time than to Morris Jones of Llanddyfnan who was probably born about 1665.

---

[26] Penrhos Papers I, 1392.
[27] Penrhos Papers I, 1392, 1766.
[28] Penrhos Papers III, 28.

There are no records at Llanddyfnan nor at Pentraeth, as early as that date. Neither are there Land Tax Assessments Lists before the 18th century. Such Tithes Apportionments records which exist are again, for a much later period.

However, there was much material among the Penrhos Papers which concerned the later forebears and a good deal of fascinating reading lay ahead!

CHAPTER 8

From different sources we learn more about many members
of this large family

THE family tree now rose to a modest height, — eight generations above my own, and ten above my grandchildren's.

The tree now also bore several other branches, — the
descendants of the other five children of Ty'n Pwll. As I
added these collateral branches, I felt that many of the
' twigs ' on these branches were to me simply names, faceless
people about whom I wanted to know more. What happened
to all those children of William and Catherine of Ty'n Pwll?

Looking over the pedigree, I realised that from before
1700 until 1860 nearly all my forebears had been tenants on
the Penrhos estate on Holy Island. Even after 1860, very
many of them were still tenants of farms and houses until
the estate was finally sold in 1944 after two lots of death
duties had been paid in rapid succession. All tenants were
given the opportunity to buy the farms, houses or shops they
were renting. The Penrhos Estate papers, covering a period
from 1403 to 1944 were all deposited in the Department of
Manuscripts and Records at the University College of North
Wales, Bangor. To these papers I returned with renewed
interest, to discover all I could about the tenants who were
my forebears. Land Tax Assessments Lists and Tithes
Apportionments Lists as well as various notes in the St. Cybi
Registers also helped to imbue these mere names with life.

Of William Hughes, Ty'n Pwll, I learned a good deal,
because he became Land Steward to Sir John Thomas
Stanley and records remain of some of his activities. Like

his father, William of Llys-y-gwynt, and his grandfather, Hugh Morris, he was also a good churchman and his name appears more than once among the list of Churchwardens, as does that of his son-in-law, William Jones, who succeeded him at Ty'n Pwll.

William, Ty'n Pwll, had at first farmed a few acres at Bodwradd and two quillets of the Ty'n Pwll land. Bodwradd, near the present Porthdafarch Road was at that time used as a posthouse, providing changes of horses for the mail coach which would be on the last lap of its long journey from London — coming from Four Mile Bridge, through Towyn Capel (now known as Trearddur Bay) and on to Porthdafarch. From here it would turn east to pass near Bodwradd and then on to the terminus, — the town of Holyhead. After the death of the tenant of Ty'n Pwll, Elin Jones, a widow in 1794, William Hughes was given the tenancy of this farm.[29] So he was gradually adding to his acres. By now he had five sons, his daughter, Elizabeth, being born the following year. His wife, Catherine, died in 1799 after the birth of a third daughter, Catherine, the infant also dying. William was left with six young children, William, the eldest being only twelve years old, and his youngest child, Elizabeth, barely four.

We can only wonder how William managed to bring up his young family, and no evidence survives to tell us about his domestic arrangements. We know from his will, and from an entry in the St. Cybi Registers that he had an illegitimate daughter, Mary, by Catherine Hughes in 1808. In several of the wills read, it was interesting to see that a son or daughter did not receive his or her share of the estate until the age of thirteen was reached. This stipulation appears in the will of William, Ty'n Pwll, — his illegitimate daughter, Mary, being eight years old when the will was signed and only twelve when her father died in 1820. This custom may be a relic of the old Welsh tribal custom

---

[29] His name appears for the first time in the Land Tax Assessment Lists for Ty'n Pwll, in 1794.

whereby a son, at thirteen, left his father's house, was provided with cattle and land from the tribal territory and became an adult, assuming all rights in the tribal settlement. By the time of William, Ty'n Pwll, I suppose the money would be considered useful for entering upon an apprenticeship for some trade or profession.

In 1809, William married a widow, Elin Zabulon, who was evidently a good wife and a kind mother to his children, for, as we have seen, she was remembered generously in his will. After the death of his father in 1810, William added the land of Llys-y-gwynt to the acres he was already farming. The house, Llys-y-gwynt, ceased to be a farmhouse and was let to Captain William Goddard who had formerly rented Quiet Corner. From time to time, Llys-y-gwynt was enlarged, and today it is a very well run Old People's Home, in the centre of a new housing estate, Morawelon. William's successors gradually added to the acres being farmed, as tenancies became vacant throughout the nineteenth century.

William of Ty'n Pwll obviously led a very busy life. Quite apart from running his own farm, he was constantly visiting other parts of Anglesey, on Penrhos affairs, and playing his part on the parochial church council.

In delving into the lives of the forebears, it was inevitable that I began to learn more about the family at Penrhos.

When I first met them in the late seventeenth and early eighteenth century papers, the Owens were landlords at Penrhos. In 1763 Sir John Thomas Stanley, baronet, of Alderley, Cheshire (1735-1807) married Margaret Owen (1742-1816), heiress of Hugh Owen of Penrhos. In a letter written to a friend, in October 1815, Madame Piozzi, formerly Mrs. Thrale, friend of Dr. Johnson, writes of Lady Stanley, now in her early seventies, as follows: "We have an old beauty come here to Bath — you can scarce remember her — one of the very much admired women, Lady Stanley. Her wit and pleasantry seem but little impaired, but the loss of health sent her here, and she wonders to see mine so good."

By January 1816, Lady Stanley is very ill, and an urgent message is sent to her son, Sir John Thomas Stanley in Cheshire that his mother wishes to see him. He set off at cnce, but did not see her alive. Lady Stanley seems to have had a foreboding of death even before her journey to Bath, for before going she had spent two whole days burning letters.

Her son, born in 1776, had succeeded to the baronetcy in 1807 and was created Lord Stanley of Alderley in 1839. His upbringing and education had been in many ways different from that of boys of his position in society at that time. His mother had strong views about her son's education and her wishes were carried out. He was taken early from school to travel under the care of a tutor, Mr. Six. Before he was twenty he had moved in the Court circles of three European capitals, Brunswick, Turin and Rome. He spoke French fluently, also German and Italian, and his love of German literature never left him. In 1789, he sailed for Iceland in his own ship, the ' John ', an enterprise then almost unprecedented. His journals and drawings remain to tell the story of his adventures in the North. He was a strong Liberal and stood alone among the Cheshire squires of his time. Fox hunting, their chief occupation and topic had little attraction for him. The character that emerges from this description undoubtedly owed much to the influence of his Welsh mother, and made him acceptable to his Welsh tenantry.

Account books, various note-books and letters in the Penrhos collection reveal a good deal of everyday life in the town of Holyhead and the whole parish and much of this would affect the life of my own people. From my work on the Penrhos Papers I had already formed the impression that the Owens and later, the Stanleys, were good landlords, showing genuine concern for and interest in their tenantry.

All property was kept in good repair; again and again in the Rental Lists appears a note that a widowed tenant would in future pay a reduced rent, or even live rent free. All they built in Holyhead, added dignity to the town. Sir John

Stanley said in a letter, " I would that this same Holyhead was not so shivered and toped about in little properties; I want a square or at least a broad street and water and garden ground for every dwelling ".[30] When one considers the perfection of the early nineteenth century Tremadoc, created by the landowner, Maddocks, with the help of his capable Welsh ' clerk of the works ' (an ex-gardener of the Marquess of Anglesey), one could imagine that the Penrhos family might have achieved the same perfection in Holyhead, had they been the only land-owners in the island! Miss Lucy Williams of Holyhead from her far more extensive reading of the Penrhos Papers has gained exactly the same impression of the Owens at Penrhos and writes of them: " The letters of three Anglesey-bred chatelaines of Penrhos, Anne Owen (née Wynne of Bodwryd), Margaret Owen (née Bold of Beaumaris and Bodwina) and Lady Stanley (née Margaret Owen, and the heiress to the combined estates of Penrhos and those of five Anglesey heiresses) as well as being direct evidence of life throughout the century, are a fair and attractive picture of the Welsh mind. They are written in English, with occasional idioms derived straight from the ' mam iaith ',[31] but the psychology is Welsh to the core and neither the society routine of London, nor her travels on the Continent altered the personality of Lady Stanley. The Owen of Penrhos felt themselves to be tribal leaders, but also members of a tribal society in which remote cousins and the poorest toilers were part of their responsibility. The letters of all the Owens show a consistent concern for the poor and suffering. Chancellor Wynne wrote to his sister (Anne Owen) that the hungry poor of the eighteenth century had grievances and that she was right to sell the corn to them at reduced rates. The letters of all the Owens show this consistent concern, not as an act of piety, but as a natural and spontaneous reaction. Her brother described Anne Owen as ' a pack horse

[30] Penrhos Papers II, Letter 439.
[31] Mother tongue.

for carrying other people's troubles '."[32] Miss Lucy Williams compares this attitude with a rather callous remark made by William Morris in one of his letters. (Letters I 445).

When Lady Stanley was absent from Penrhos, in Cheshire or at her town house in London, there was evidently frequent correspondence between her and Robert Roberts, a schoolmaster in Holyhead who seems to have acted as her confidential secretary. It is a great pity that only five of these letters have survived, for they make delightful reading.

Robert Roberts who is usually referred to as Almanaciwr (Almanack-maker) died on August 3rd, 1836, aged 58, and below these particulars on his tombstone in St. Cybi's Churchyard is inscribed "Awdur y Daearyddiaeth." His letters not only keep Lady Stanley in touch with all that is happening at Penrhos, but also give her news of what is going on in the town, and of any ills that may have befallen her tenants. He has a sense of humour, and his occasional classical references are very happily phrased. His grammar and syntax are impeccable except on rare occasions, when his pupils interrupt him or he is in a hurry to finish a letter. These are letters from a servant to his employer, but in them we find no servility or obsequiousness.

Early in my own experience and knowledge of Welsh people I had become aware again and again of this lowering of the barriers between people of very different social status. A man or woman in a humble occupation had dignity and ease of manner when encountering those who might be assumed to be very much his or her superior in position, wealth and education. I first became conscious of this attractive trait in the Welsh, in the first World War, when we returned to Anglesey to live, and recognised it again later, when I went to live in Merioneth. I also learned that the most humble of Welshmen knew well and could quote extensively from the literature of their country, even from that of earliest times. George Borrow comments on this

[32] Transactions of the Anglesey Antiquarian Society, 1950.

attribute of the Welsh in 'Wild Wales', saying that one would never meet an English peasant who could discuss Chaucer or Spenser, but it was quite common to find a Welsh weaver or quarryman who would discuss Medieval Welsh literature with him.

Is the ease of communication between people of different social classes a survival of the old Welsh tribal system where the settlement or village was the home of one tribe or family? Certainly, in the late eighteenth century, one could find the squire, i.e., the head of the tribe, in the manor house; a brother might be the rector; another brother might be the miller; another brother the innkeeper, and so on. And so, in the eighteenth century Bryn Ddu diaries, we have William Bulkely, the Squire, acknowledging not only kinship but friendship with a glazier whom he calls 'my friend and nephew, Owen Williams, the glazier at Llanerchymedd'. Again and again he makes frequent kindly references to his humble kinsmen, 'Mary Evans, being my poor relation'.

But I am digressing, and must return to Robert Roberts. It is evident that the schoolmaster not only kept Lady Stanley in touch with affairs at home but also undertook a certain amount of financial responsibility. We learn many interesting details about wages paid, expenses incurred and accounts settled, and we learn the current prices for everyday commodities.

" The Captains of the Post Office packets at the end of the 18th century and early 19th century were ex-naval officers who had seen service in the long war with France and were a valuable accession to local social life. The best known name among these was that of Captain J. McGregor Skinner who was in command of a sailing packet cutter on this station (Holyhead) and from 1821 to 1832 of the steam packets."[33]

If there was a very large bill to be met, Robert Roberts was evidently able to call on Captain Skinner for help, but for smaller amounts, if funds ran low he used his own money

[33] Miss Lucy Williams. Transactions of the Anglesey Antiquarian Society, 1950.

which he kept in the grandfather clock in his house! The successful sale of cattle by William Hughes, the Land Steward, could also ease the financial situation for a time. And by these means, all accounts for Penrhos were paid promptly, when the family was away.

The following extract from a letter addressed to Lady Stanley in London, dated April 29th, 1809, is not without humour. He has given her various items of news of the tenants and of happenings in Holyhead one of which reads: "We have a set of strolling players doing wonders to a crowded house at the Druid Theatre." He then goes on: "thus far I may say my story has been entertaining; now I have rather an unpleasant tale to relate which is on the score of 'arian' (money). On doing the Penrhos book for May, the balance for Lady Stanley was 34£; but on closing the same for June the balance for R.R. was 36£! The principal robbers were the Felin Heli 17£; slates for Court Newydd with an overplus for reserve carried nem. con. by William Hughes, J. Williams and myself about 15£. Try Griffiths Esq. 4.10.0; Penrhos wages about 3£ per week; joiners and masons about 5£ for do., with the accustomed odds and ends. I had recourse to Mrs. Williams and to a clock club treasury in my own house till I had orders to go to Captain Skinner, when his donation of 60£ (to be paid to Davision & Co., Pall Mall) settled Mrs. Williams and the treasury, besides the many bills which were in want of being cashed. But I am sorry to add that the 60£ are nearly gone and I must again have recourse to the treasury or somewhere else."[34]

In a letter dated August 17th, 1812, Roberts passes on a message from the Land Steward: "William Hughes wishes to know by the next letter are the cattle of three years old at Penrhos and Tre Gof to be sold; if they are, it will be necessary to know immediately as the *prime* fairs will soon be over." He apologises for carelessness in writing: "I am sorry to say I am interrupted every two minutes whilst writing this, by my pupils, of course its errors in statements

[34] Penrhos Papers 1640.

68

are many." He concludes: "It is expected that the ale at Penrhos will last till the beginning of the hay harvest, exclusive of Richard's strong corn barrel reserved for your Ladyship's happy return. Mr. L. Owen will supply a barrel or two for that *dry* period . . . Expecting to hear soon, I subscribe myself Your Ladyship's humble servant, Robt. Roberts."[35]

In another letter dated September 3rd, 1812, the writer again refers to a temporary shortage of money, to settle Penrhos accounts. "My principal reason for writing at present is to inform your Ladyship that my purse was on last Monday quite drained of all its contents, in consequence of the conjunction of the Garreg Domas plasterer's and the Forge mason's bills so that I was obliged to visit Captain Skinner who immediately said that any sum that was requisite would accommodate him as well as myself; he of course advised me to take 50£ which is to be paid to Mr. Davison as before. The following day William Hughes brought me 21£ odd for the toll corn at Felin Heli, therefore I am confident that I shall trouble your Ladyship no more on the score of *arian* till after your safe arrival at Penrhos." He continues by talking of the harvest, — "Our harvest is now universal; the crop is reckoned good, and better weather we never enjoyed, as we have had not a drop of rain for the last fortnight. I was at Penrhos last night; the harvest there goes on well, and another fortnight of fine weather would entitle the labourers to sing harvest home. John Williams is the only invalid there, his leg being rather bad still, but not to prevent his walking to town every night contrary to my preaching to him. Dinam (one of the Penrhos horses) is recovering fast, and little Wousky seems to be in very good spirits." This long letter ends with a slightly satirical comment on arrangements lately introduced for signalling to the packet boat.

"The improvements at the flag staff in Captain Fellowes's garden are still increasing. There are now eight or ten

[35] Penrhos Papers 1642.

colours: one to order the packet back to the bay; another to order it to sail immediately; a third to order it to return; a fourth to order the mate immediately to the office, etc., etc.! Blue lights also, are preparing to give similar orders during the approaching winter nights. The consequence of this is the eyes of the packet from the arrival of the mail, to its passing the Head are henceforth to be fixed on the above named pole. Such arbitrary despotic extremes make some declaim 'The world at last is mad with its novelties.'

I shall expect to hear from your Ladyship in a few days, till then I beg leave to remain Your Ladyship's devoted and humble servant, Robert Roberts."[36]

Enclosures of the common land were, of course, still in progress throughout Anglesey and it seems apparent that when a piece of land was enclosed, a prospective tenant would be provided with all materials for the building of a farmhouse, or house. He would clear the ground and then presumably would begin to pay rent. Evidence of this procedure appears more than once in the Penrhos Papers. There are still people in Holyhead who can say which land had long ago been common land. William Hughes, the Land Steward, evidently as part of his duties, would carry out these arrangements and report to Lady Stanley, or in her absence to Robert Roberts. In a letter dated 20th October, 1815, we read:

"Two of the poorest steers at Penrhos were sold last week for 9£ a head, ready money. W. Hughes after conveying them to Llangefni called at Rhosymeirch, where he saw a neat slated cottage built by Hugh Williams. Others who had portions of your Ladyship's allotment of that common were preparing, but no foundations were yet laid."[37]

This letter also gives a vivid and dramatic description of stormy weather off Holyhead.

"The herring fishery is beginning to be pretty good; two or three hundred a net are caught. This morning was very

[36] Penrhos Papers 1643.
[37] Penrhos Papers 1644.

tempestuous; two boats had gone out at five, about an hour previous to the hurricane which at six began with similar fury to that of December 7th last year. Every eye was directed to the two boats; one got in at Porthmaenmarch, but the other having William Thomas, Marchog, and others equally clumsy to manage was at intervals seen drifting to the offing, in spite of all their efforts. At length and when the tempest was in its utmost fury, eight veterans roused by feelings of humanity manned a long boat with eight oars and pushed to the deep, and with the swiftness of a meteor over mountainous waves they soon reached the unfortunate boat which they with much labour and toil succeeded in towing safe ashore! Wind S.W."

How well I know that South West wind which seems to blow two days out of three in Holyhead.

He continues to tell of the damage wrought by the storm and ends his letter:

" The post being about to close, I must end my story. I hope your Ladyship continues to enjoy good health and that the healing waters of Bath may be truly beneficial. With best respects to Mrs. Higonette (Lady Stanley's maid) I remain Your Ladyship's devoted servant, Robert Roberts."

There is another letter, headed: Holyhead, July 4th (Saturday), 1812, which must be quoted in part, not only because of the reference to William Hughes who is now farming the land of Llys-y-gwynt as well as that of Ty'n Pwll, but because of the delightful way in which the writer refers to the improved weather effected by the changes of the moon. His reference to the working horses at Penrhos is equally happy.

" The hay harvest at Penrhos commenced June 29th; the additional labourers are William Rowland, late of Ty'n Towyn; Jo. Hughes Penybryn and Wm. Hughes, Llys-y-gwynt.[38] It was thought till last Thursday that they would be obliged to desist owing to continual rains, but Madam

[38] Perhaps his eldest son, William (1787-1876).

Luna having since that period laid her wet masque aside and promised faithfully (as far as it respects Wales) not to resume it till she changes, they are going briskly on, hoping by then to have a good part of it in Cyrnini.

John Davies, the Coachman, with his favourites Doctor and Dinam are equally faithful in carrying gravel to the roads about Penrhos, old Jack is also faithful when called upon, which is but seldom but old Zaby is daily employed, and is in excellent spirits; the remainder of the cavalry are also enjoying good health. Monsrs. Rory and Frank are the same as before but poor Wousky is but indifferent."[39]

Further on a little gaiety in the town is mentioned: " A grand ball is to take place at Garreg Domas on the 17th inst. when a great number of our townsfolk from the *prime* to the principals of the middle class are to assemble; musicians from Dublin are to attend. I had this information last night of Mr. Brown . . ."

Every kind of news is given at length, — a little Irish roguery over horse dealing; the crew of a certain Captain Davies being dismissed " for having each a good deal of salt on board "; a sad tale of an " English servant maid who proved pregnant of Ned Lloyd (an Englishman) the driver of the Chester mail . . . Lloyd was forced to marry immediately with very apparent signs of its being against his will."[40]

Robert Roberts, in fact, says in one of the letters that he keeps a record of all that was going on in the town and at Penrhos, and this news is included in the next letter. References to the weather are, of course, frequent because of the importance of good weather to work being carried out, so again in a letter dated August 17th, 1812, we read:

" As my epistle generally commences with remarks on a harvest, I have to state that another important *one* is brought in at Penrhos after the hay viz.: the *Mawn;** having had no rain for the last six weeks, they were perfectly dry. The corn

---

[39] Penrhos Papers 1641.
[40] Penrhos Papers 1641.
* Peat, sometimes referred to in leases as ' turffe ' or 'sods '.

comes on remarkably well; they begin to cut in some parts of the island, but not yet in our parish."

Another collection of letters among the Penrhos Papers also reveal a good deal of life at Penrhos and events in the town of Holyhead in the late eighteenth and early nineteenth centuries. I had read these many years before, and now I could picture my newly- found forebears against this background.[41]

William, as Land Steward, was undoubtedly able to exercise a little nepotism! His family, too, had been tenants on the Penrhos Estate for over a hundred years and he would doubtless be well-liked and trusted. When William, Llys-y-gwynt, had died in 1810, the tenancy of 'Yr Efail Bach' was granted to his grandson, another William Hughes, the eldest son of Ty'n Pwll. On March 18th, 1812, William of 'Yr Efail Bach' married Jane Jones, spinster, in St. Cybi's Church. They had twelve children, eight of whom survived infancy and childhood. They later went to live in Holyhead and their son, John, born in 1828, farmed 'Yr Efail Bach'.

William Hughes, 'Yr Efail Bach', was a very well-known figure in Holyhead and lived to be eighty-nine. In 1815, he was appointed Parish Clerk and the story of his appointment has been recorded by Chancellor Briscoe who became Vicar of Holyhead in 1857. He had had the full story from William Hughes himself.

An entry in the vestry book *9th March, 1841*, reads: 'Resolved unanimously that William Hughes be re-elected Parish Clerk of this parish and also a Sexton for ye same terms as he held the same and said offices heretofore'. In 1861, Chancellor Briscoe had evidently read the 1841 note, and perhaps wondered why William had been "re-elected." Hearing what William had to say, Chancellor Briscoe left the following note: *20th November, 1861.* "William Hughes this day informs me 'that ye circumstances that led to this were his having had some words with the Incumbent and saying to him — 'Well, nid oes dim am dani ondi my ymadael

[41] Edited by Miss Jane Henrietta Adeane, a descendant of Sir John and Lady Stanley.

galangenaf '.[42] He likewise tells me that he had his original appointment as Clerk from Lady Stanley who told him to go and act as Clerk — that the Incumbent winced (wingar).[43] considerably at this and said the appointment belonged to him, but that by the persuasion of a Mr. Griffith, he was induced to acquiesce in it; this was in 1815." William remained Parish Clerk until his death in 1876 at the age of eighty-nine, and must have been present at baptisms, marriages and burials of dozens of his relatives.

In 1866 several old residents of Holyhead were called to give evidence in a case brought by the London & North Western Railway Company, claiming relief of payments of rates. " William Hughes, Parish Clerk of Holyhead, was then called and sworn. He said he was eighty years old and had been Parish Clerk since 1815. Never known the boundaries but had heard his grandfather say that Madam Owen of Penrhos used formerly to have some boundaries walked." He continues by describing Holyhead as it was when he was a boy.

The second son of William Hughes (1761-1820) was Hugh Hughes born at Tre Gof on January 18th, 1789.[44] Tre Gof was the home farm on the Penrhos Estate and it is evident that William Hughes had already begun his duties as Land Steward to the Stanleys, this being his first home after his marriage in 1786. It was pleasantly situated, facing the stretch of water separating Holy Island from Anglesey and less than a mile from Penrhos itself. The house is now derelict.

Hugh Hughes (1789-1869), later became tenant of Ty Mawr Mynydd. This had originally been part of the largest farm on the island, two hundred and eighteen acres farmed for two or three generations by a family named Rogers. It was even then known as Ty Mawr Mynydd.[45] At that time

[42] Well, the only thing I can do is to clear out.
[43] Wingar. Perhaps ' bridled ' or showed resentment, would be a better translation.
[44] Note left among the papers of Hugh Hughes 1789-1869.
[45] Penrhos Papers I, 1392.

it was mostly moorland and uncultivated land. The Rogers ceased to farm there soon after 1790,[46] Hugh Rogers dying in 1784, and when his widow gave up farming, the land was evidently cut up and smaller farms created, for new farmhouse names appear in the rental lists, and new tenants. Hugh Hughes first appears as tenant of Ty Mawr Mynydd in 1817 and his was probably the original and oldest farmhouse in the area. In 1814, he married Mary, daughter of Richard Williams, farmer of Llanfihangel-yn-Nhowyn, and when they went to Ty Mawr Mynydd, they already had one daughter, Elizabeth, their son, William, being born in 1817. It is interesting to follow events on the farm, by way of the annual rental lists. In 1817 Hugh has seventy-nine acres, but as the land is cultivated and his stock increases there is evidently need for more farm buildings. In 1826 we find the following entry in the Rental books for the years 1821-1827; " *1826* Hugh Hughes, Ty Mawr Mynydd, £35. The tenant has built in addition to the house a barn, stables, cowhouse well worth £90 towards which he was allowed timber, slate, stone line valued at £50 ".[47] By 1852 his rental is £41 and his two sons, Thomas and Hugh Hughes are renting adjoining farms Gorsgoch and Porth-y-Gwyddel for a rental of £34.8.6 with an allowance of 10/6 for draining some of the land.

Hugh, like his father and grandfather, was also a good churchman. When one considers the distance from Ty Mawr Mynydd into the town of Holyhead, and the lack of proper roads in those days, one wonders at the regular church attendance of people from outlying farms. Hugh would, of course, go on horseback, and when the children were old enough to go, there doubtless would be a pony and trap. Towards the end of the century, the roads improved, but one has only to look at maps of the area even as late as 1850, to visualise the difficulties not only of the churchgoer, but for the farmer who had to bring his produce in to market, or his animals to the various cattle fairs.

[46] Penrhos Papers I, 1392.
[47] Penrhos Papers II, 72.

75

Hugh was a churchwarden and a member of the parish vestry, and at one time was responsible for keeping the accounts of the Poor Rate — relief then being in the hands of the Church. A small black notebook has survived, labelled Poor Rate Book, September 1828. Hugh Hughes has written his name and the address of Ty Mawr Mynydd, South Stack, on the inside of the cover. The poor rate for that year was 6d. in the £, and the book lists those who pay the rate. Sir John Thomas Stanley heads the list with £6.12.7. and some householders pay as little as 4d. Hugh's contribution was 18/1½.

Hugh's eldest son, William (1817-1904) left home to become a sailor, his home port being Liverpool. In 1841 through the good offices of the Hon. Edward Stanley he was appointed Customs Official in Liverpool. Late in 1856 he emigrated to America and farmed in Davenport, Iowa. He kept in close touch with his kinsmen in Holyhead and was later joined by his niece and nephews, Mary, Hugh and John Jones, children of his sister Margaret. Mary Jones remained with her uncle until her marriage to James Sherwood Bell in 1870. Hugh Jones died of cholera at the age of nineteen and his brother John became a farmer at Ruthven, Iowa.

William Hughes prospered, leaving just over $51,000, and as he remained unmarried, many of his Anglesey kinsmen were generously remembered in his will, — his sister, Mary, who by that time had succeeded her father as tenant of Ty Mawr Mynydd, first cousins, John Hughes and Elizabeth Hughes at Yr Efail Bach, his first cousin Ann Grace Hughes (1831-1911), as well as first cousins on his mother's side, Elizabeth and Owen Williams. Property and money were left to his local Baptist Church and to St. Luke's Hospital in Iowa. In the third codicil of the will, signed on July 18th, 1902, he bequeaths money to the Bangor Baptist Theological College, North Wales.

Hugh's second son, Richard, was born in 1819, went to sea and became a master mariner. His mother was buried in the lower burial ground of St. Cybi's Church in 1856 and on

76

her gravestone we read: " Captain Richard Hughes, son of Hugh and Mary Hughes, Ty Mawr, South Stack, who lost his life by the capsizing of his vessel during a hurricane in Humboldt Bay on passage from San Francisco to Clamach River. Born 10th October, 1819." Under this is written: " Mary, wife of Hugh Hughes, died 16th June, 1856, aged 66."

In 1849, Richard, by now an experienced mariner had joined the Gold Rush to California but after several months decided he could make a more certain living in his original profession. The letter in which he tells his father of his experiences is vividly written and some of the words with which he speaks of his resolve to leave the diggings and return to sea are almost biblical. " Laterly (sic) I have had charge of a small Vessel Running in the Bays and Rivers Freighting which I find myself better Talented for than for Digging and as Profitable. I spent 2½ months in the Mines . . . All a Lottery . . . Myself I resolved matters over, examined my Dust [gold] and found it wanting." He had after this prospered and had evidently intended to settle in Iowa as a farmer, for he had earlier bought land there and in 1842 had become an American citizen. At his death in 1853, this land came to his father, Hugh Hughes, and it was some of this which was later farmed by the eldest brother, William, when he emigrated late in 1856.

Hugh's third son, Hugh Hugh Hughes, gave up farming at Porth-y-Gwyddel and went to Australia early in 1854 during the gold rush. He was not successful in finding gold, but after initial hardships prospered as a builder, soon employing his own workmen. He later returned to Holyhead and died at 14 London Road, in 1893.

Hugh and Mary Hughes's eldest daugther, Elizabeth, made a very late marriage in January 1856 to John Roberts, a Liverpool builder, aged 65. By that time he had already built a good deal of property at the south end of Liverpool in the area then known as Toxteth Park, but these houses have now gone and are replaced by new Liverpool Cor-

77

poration property. Elizabeth has contributed several letters to the family correspondence and reveals herself as an anxious and affectionate daughter and sister.

Hugh and Mary's next child was Margaret, born in 1823. In 1847, she married John Jones, Lightkeeper at South Stack Lighthouse. They farmed Plas Nico, less than a mile from the lighthouse. John Jones (1819-1859), Plas Nico, was the son of John Jones, Ty Mawr, Penrhosfeilw, the first Lightkeeper at the then new South Stack Lighthouse. Like so many Lightkeepers of their day they were also small farmers, the elder John Jones appearing in Penrhos Rental Lists in 1817, 1827, farming twenty-six acres, and again in 1841 in Tithes Apportionments Lists.

In 1878, Margaret Jones, now a widow, is still at Plas Nico where she remained until her death in 1893. The six surviving children of this marriage are the grandchildren mentioned in the will of Hugh, Ty Mawr Mynydd. A study of the Ty Mawr Mynydd pedigree (page 40) gives further information of these six grandchildren, but the William Jones 1858-1940 is the one most familiar to me, as I had heard his name mentioned so often. He is, of course, the father of my newly-found cousin, Freda. From what I have now learned of him from her, I wish I had known him, for like so many of the Hughes family, he seems to have been an excellent father in every way, showing affection for and interest in his children and concerned that they should speak good Welsh. This attribute I have recognised in many of the Hughes descendants.

Thomas (1826-1888) made several attempts to find congenial work outside Anglesey. He writes from Runcorn; we hear he has gone to Dublin; and finally to London. He evidently decided Anglesey was the best place for him and returned home to farm Gors Goch, near Ty Mawr Mynydd. He eventually married but had no children.

John, the youngest son (1835- ?) spent two sessions in Liverpool at the Mechanics' Institution, where he studied surveying and what he describes in a letter "mapping in."

He seems to have been a lively, high-spirited boy, irked by the discipline at home. The family letters suggest that he finally left home on this account, went to America, sending the family very little news of his doings. His father remembers him, when making his will, but has to say " to my son John, wherever he is."

Hugh Hughes, Ty Mawr Mynydd, died in 1869 and was succeeded at the farm by his unmarried daugther, Mary, 1829-1916. Mary Hughes is remembered affectionately by her great-niece, Freda, who always experienced great happiness on her frequent visits, as a child to Ty Mawr Mynydd. There is some special quality about the friendship and affection which can develop between a small child and a very elderly relative as I know from my own experience with my Welsh grandmother and even more in the affection I had for my old great-aunt Greenough of whom I must write later on. I was delighted when Freda gave me a beautiful sampler worked by "Mary Hughes, her work " when she was a child. It is a coincidence that I have been able to hang it alongside another sampler of mid-Victorian origin worked by one Anne Roberts of Barmouth, born in 1851. Anne Roberts married Owen Elias and eventually lived in Plas Penrhosfeiliw, outside Holyhead. She was my father-in-law's first cousin, and Freda tells me she was sometimes taken to Plas, to tea by her Aunt Mary, and always remembered seeing the peacocks and the pug dog. And now the samplers of the two friends hang side by side in my house! Mary Hughes was succeeded at the farm by her eldest niece, Elizabeth Jones, Freda's aunt, who remained there until 1937. She was then ninety and her people quite rightly considered she should give up farming, and she left Ty Mawr Mynydd. The tenure of this family at Ty Mawr Mynydd was from 1814 to 1937.

We must now leave Hugh and his descendants and turn to my direct forebear, Thomas, the gardener, born in 1791. Why did Thomas never become a farmer? Did he not wish this, or was there no farm available for him at the right time? Perhaps he became a gardener, while waiting for a suitable farm to be available. He may have been happy in his work at the Royal Hotel and quite content to remain there. He would have about four acres of land under his care, and no doubt as he became experienced would become the head gardener, with assistants. I can remember the Hotel gardens, as they were called, very well indeed, for at the beginning of the century they extended for about four acres behind Rostrevor, my grandparents' home. The hotel for which the gardens provided vegetables and fruit by that time, was of course the comparatively new large Station Hotel.

Thomas lived at 10 Mill Street,[48] one of the houses left to him by his father, William Hughes, Ty'n Pwll, and remained here all his life.[49] After paying out the sums due to his brothers, William, James and Richard, under the terms of their father's will, Thomas would have a fair income. We must assume that he was reliable and practical for the management of the property to have been entrusted to his care. He was evidently thrifty and capable for we know he owned three houses in Porth-y-felin which in 1856 he wished to sell for £180. They are leasehold, the lease having another 68 years to run.[50]

It cannot be said he took any active part in Church work; his duties at the Royal Hotel would prevent that and may also have been responsible for the apparent carelessness about the christenings of his children. We know little of his wife, Grace, but she was literate, her signature appearing in the Marriage Register with that of her husband. I was later to learn that she was born in Cheshire.[51] To her I must owe my third Christian name which passed to me from the grand-daughter of the original Grace! I wonder if she is represented among some of those handsome women in Do's 'Welsh box'! We shall never know. When Thomas became elderly, he

[48] Off Thomas Street, part of Mill Street is now known as Ucheldre Ave.
[49] Census Returns 1841, 1851, 1861.
[50] Family letter dated January 15th, 1856.
[51] Census Returns 1861.

became the Hall Porter at the old Royal Hotel, in its early days a coaching inn, and as this he is described on his death certificate.

I wonder if he may have welcomed George Borrow on his arrival at the Royal Hotel when he stayed there in 1854, although the latter seems to have been in one of his truculent moods when he arrived there. Perhaps he was tired after his long tramp across Anglesey that day, in the course of which he had visited the home of Owen Tudor. Of his entrance to the town, George Borrow writes:

"I doubled my pace which was before tolerably quick, and soon saw a noble edifice on my left, brilliantly lighted up. 'What a capital inn that would make' said I, looking at it wistfully, as I passed it. Presently I found myself in the midst of a poor, dull, ill-lighted town.

'Where is the inn?' said I to a man.

'The inn, Sir; you have passed it. The inn is younder', he continued, pointing to the noble-looking edifice."

Borrow turned back, entered the hotel. 'Send Boots' I roared to the waiter, as I flung myself down in an arm-chair in a magnificent coffee-room. 'What the deuce are you staring at? Send Boots, can't you, and ask what I can have for dinner.' Before long, he and the Boots whom Borrow describes as a "grey-haired venerable-looking man" were soon deep in discussion on Welsh poets, particularly Goronwy Owen, and talking about Lewis Morris, one of the three gifted Anglesey brothers.

Borrow says he "dined or rather supped well at the inn, — I beg its pardon, Hotel, for the word Inn at the present day is decidedly vulgar. I likewise slept well; how could I do otherwise, passing the night, as I did, in an excellent bed in a large, cool quiet room."

Most of the hotel has now disappeared; what remains has been converted into houses which are still dignified in appearance.

Thomas died in September 1862, at the Royal Hotel, not at Mill Street. He must have been taken ill suddenly, for he died of pneumonia after five days' illness, and was buried in St. Seiriol's Churchyard. His death was registered by his elder daughter, Ann Grace Hughes of 8 Swift Square. The square is said to be named after Dean Swift who once spent seven tedious days in the tall old inn there, waiting for a favourable wind to take his ship to Dublin, but it is more likely to have been named after a Postmaster of that name who was stationed at Holyhead in Cromwell's day. It has been suggested that Dean Swift was in fact a kinsman of the Cromwellian postmaster but perhaps did not care to acknowledge the connection! Only three or four of these houses still remain, and it is no longer a square. The inn and adjoining house had in medieval days been one building and both were demolished during the second World War. They had become unsafe after a bomb had been dropped nearby. From what was discovered at that time it seemed evident that the inn and house had originally been the site of the old monastic buildings attached to the Collegiate Church of St. Cybi.

In September 1862, Ann Grace would be thirty-one, and the two eldest motherless daughters of her brother William had been living with her for nearly six years, and she presumably was still Headmistress of the National School. Responsibilities had descended early upon her.

Thomas signed his will on September 12th, 1862, three days before his death. The signature is that of a very ill man who can scarcely hold the pen. Two of the witnesses to the will are his brother, Hugh Hughes of Ty Mawr, Holyhead, and Robert Prichard, Auctioneer, of Holyhead. His brother-in-law, William Jones, Ty'n Pwll, is appointed "executor in trust of this my will and guardian for my said daughters."

His wife is left the leasehold house "with the appurtenances thereto belonging, situate in Mill Street, Holyhead," during her life. His daughters, Ann Grace Hughes and Catherine, wife of Robert Parry are each left a house in Cross Street. The residue and remainder of his real and personal estate is devised and bequeathed to his two daughters absolutely as tenants in common and not as joint tenants.

His wife, Grace, his son, William who had made his home with his parents in his widowerhood and his two daughters were each left £30. Of Thomas, the eldest son, there is no mention. He had left Holyhead in the 1840's to become a Customs Official in Liverpool and had perhaps lost touch with the family. Grace Hughes died on March 8th, 1877, aged 78; her daughter, Catherine Parry died in 1893.

Of the twin sons of Ty'n Pwll, little has been discovered. James became a shoemaker and lived in Blackridge. In the St. Cybi Registers are registered the baptisms of his five children, Richard, Ann, Hugh, Margaret and William. It is disappointing not to know more about him. Perhaps one of his sons became a nonconformist minister and was a good preacher, or a daughter became a schoolmistress, or married a well-to-do shopkeeper. We might have discovered a singer or writer! But these are idle surmises.

Of this twin, Richard, I learned a little more. He went to sea and became a master mariner. He died in 1852 when his youngest child was four. His wife, Grace, died in 1870, being buried in St. Seiriol's Churchyard with her daughter, Elizabeth (1840-1907) and son-in-law, Richard Jones (1840-1898). The name of Captain Richard Hughes appears from time to time in the Penrhos Estate accounts. In 1819 he was paid " 12/- for freight of a piano to Liverpool " and we find on " May 24th, 1821, Captain Richard Hughes, freight and duty, coal and bricks, £10.4.6."[52]

These accounts kept by Robert Roberts are interesting in revealing current prices of various commodities in the years 1811-1821. We find a bottle of ink, 1/-; for thatching a house, 14/-; 21 tons of coal, duty and freight, £28.9.7; three bills to Mr. Jones, Druggist, £11.2.3.

On August 26th, 1812, there is £2.2.0 paid to William Hughes (Land Steward) for labourers' work at Penrhos. In November of the same year William Hughes is paid £55.15.0.

[52] Penrhos Papers I, 1438.

for timber (presumably supplied to various farms for repairs or extension to buildings).

In 1813, a donation and subscription to the Bible Society £6.6.0. from Penrhos. (This was a yearly item).

In August 1813 — freight of slates from Caernarvon to Capt. W. Parry £13.12.0.

Six months after the death of William Hughes, Ty'n Pwll, we find this entry: February 3rd, 1821, to Executors of late William Hughes £20.4.0½.[53]

Captain Richard Hughes married Grace Ellis in 1824.[54] They had nine children and it is interesting to find from the Penrhos Rental Lists that Richard and Grace moved house almost every other year! And from one end of the town to the other! Had I unlimited time, I should try to trace all their descendants, but one I did manage to follow down the tree, simply because of a remark I had heard once or twice, in childhood. I had, of course, made a list of the children of Captain Richard Hughes, from the St. Cybi Registers to add to the family tree, beginning with his eldest son, John, born in 1825, to his last child, Edward Jones, born in 1848. Sometime later, I was working through a later period in the St. Cybi's Parish Marriage Registers, in search of the marriage of the elusive Catherine, younger daughter of Thomas the gardener. Suddenly my eyes lighted on " John Hughes, aged 30 bachelor, engineer to Ann Michael, spinster aged 29, the bridegroom's father being Richard Hughes, mariner, deceased. The bride's father was Richard Michael, mariner." The date was 29th January, 1856.

The name Ann Michael rang a very loud bell in my memory. Surely I had heard more than once that Do and my father had a ' cousin ' named Annie Michael Hughes whose sister was named Olga. There was also a brother, named John Hughes, who had a comical nickname, ' Tin Can '. He, too, was an engineer.

[53] Penrhos Papers I, 1438.
[54] St. Cybi's Parish Registers.

The next time I saw Do, I questioned her about these ' cousins '. Oh! yes, they were related to us, but how? Do was not really sure! However, she did remember that their mother had been a Miss Ann Ada Swaine and their father was John Hughes, an engineer, Do thought. She also had a vague idea of the age of Annie Michael Hughes. I had myself met her once, about 1920, she by that time being the wife of our solicitor, O. B. Edwards. I remembered her as a very charming person, but had no idea that she had once been Annie Michael Hughes! Now, having this promising clue, curiosity or perhaps a desire to know our exact relationship made me pursue further enquiries. In due course, I discovered that John Hughes, aged 25, engineer, bachelor of Upper Park Street, Holyhead, had married Ann Ada Swaine, spinster, aged 20 years of 36 Stanley Street, Holyhead. The bridegroom's father was John Hughes, engineer, deceased. The date of the marriage was July 15th, 1889. Their first child was Ann Michael Hughes, born the following year.

So here was the proof that Ann Michael Hughes and her sister and brothers were indeed third cousins to Do and my father, and, of course, to Trevor. Trevor was astonished, when I gave him this piece of news, for he had known Annie Mick, as he affectionately called her, very well indeed and had always admired her.

Later, I was to learn of the tragic death of Richard's son, Ellis, born in 1836. As his sailing ship, outward bound, was near the mouth of the Mersey, he fell from the masthead into the sea and was drowned before help could reach him. This was in 1856.

The youngest child of Ty'n Pwll was Elizabeth, 1795-1878, Trevor's great-grandmother. In May 1820, a few months before her father's death, she married William Jones of Llangeinwen, Anglesey.[55] It is possible that even a year or two before this date, William of Ty'n Pwll had been considering semi-retirement, for on December 4th, 1818, a lease

[55] St. Cybi Registers.

85

was granted by Sir John Thomas Stanley to William Hughes of Ty'n Pwll, gent., of a messuage or tenement called Ty'n-rallt,[56] for the life of the lessee for a rent of £10 annually. With this went three acres of land. Perhaps William, though only fifty-seven, envisaged this as a quiet retreat for himself and his wife Elin, with Elizabeth and her husband living at Ty'n Pwll. From Trevor, I learned exactly where Ty'n Rallt stands and was told who had lived there when Trevor and I were children, a certain Captain and Mrs. Myrtle with a daughter, Jessie. It was almost uncanny how Trevor's words brought from the depths of my memory, a vivid picture of this pretty little double-fronted house, covered with cream roses. I also had a vivid recollection of Jessie Myrtle, whom I recalled as a beautiful, dark young girl. The house is quite near Yr Efail Bach, within a few yards of the last cross-road on the A5 just half a mile before it enters Holyhead. It would in 1818 lie within a stone's throw of Ty'n Pwll which then stood where the railway now runs down the last gentle slope into Holyhead. Of course, William may not have meant to retire there himself but perhaps intended it for his daughter, Elizabeth and her future husband — but again, all this is surmise!

William Hughes died less than two years later, in September 1820, at Ty'n Pwll, aged only fifty-nine. His son-in-law, William Jones, became the next tenant of Ty'n Pwll. In the St. Cybi Registers we find his name as Churchwarden in 1827 and 1835. From the Penrhos Rental Lists we find that he gradually added to the acres he farmed, as adjacent tenancies fell vacant, so that by 1841 he was farming not only Ty'n Pwll but the land adjacent to this as well as a one acre field at Twll-y-Clawdd and thirteen acres at Cefn Coch.[57]

It was probably about this time that Ty'n Pwll was demolished, as it lay in the path of the proposed railway line

[56] Penrhos Papers III, 91-92.
[57] Tithes Apportionments List for 1841.

to Holyhead. The name of the house, of course, means house in a hollow, and that last mile or so of the railway to its terminus at Holyhead does indeed run down between fairly high embankments which to me, taking my last look at the island whenever I leave it, exasperatingly cut off from my view, familiar landmarks.

The Railway Company built a new house to replace Ty'n Pwll and this today still stands on the old Ty'n Pwll Road, but about three hundred yards from the railway. It faces South West with an open view across to the Caernarvonshire mountains, and until quite recently was Trevor's home, Ty Mawr.

William Jones and Elizabeth had nine children, five of whom survived. William, born in 1821 eventually farmed Bodwina, near Gwalchmai, and his brother, Lewis, born in 1823 farmed Llwyn Onn and became Land Agent to the Marquess of Anglesey. These were the two nephews of Hugh, Ty Mawr Mynydd, who were appointed co-trustees with Chancellor Briscoe by Hugh's will. Two daughters, Margaret and Catherine, died in childhood. Elizabeth was born in 1828, Thomas and Louisa in 1830 and 1832. Owen and Catherine were born in 1835 and 1837 respectively.

Owen married Catherine Hughes of Tregaian, near Llangefni, and succeeded his father at the farm now known as Ty Mawr. He lived there until his death in 1907, his wife living until 1939. The pedigree shows that the two daughters of this marriage married farmers, the younger daughter, Mary, marrying Richard Lloyd, farmer of Ty'n Llan and eventually becoming the mother of Trevor and his sister, Phyllis.

Trevor, in his turn farmed Ty Mawr, and now his elder son is farming Ty'n Llan and another Ty Mawr on the larger island of Anglesey, but adjacent to Ty'n Llan. Trevor, as far as my research can show, is the only one who as a descendant of this Hughes ' clan ' has remained in the family occupation — one unbroken line of farmers from about 1685 until today, to my mind almost the most desirable heredity possible.

Having nearly reached the end of this excessively long chapter, I suppose it would be fitting to mention that in the Penrhos Rental Lists of the nineteenth century appear the names of close relatives of Grace Hughes, — the person who caused this search to be made. It has already been told that her father, William, the mariner, rented a house in Station Place, where his two younger daughters were born, Grace in 1852 and Ann in 1854. After the death of his wife, Mary, he spent his time ashore, with his parents at 10 Mill Street, but I have failed to find where he lodged after 1862. His second daughter, Margaret Hughes, married William Gannon in 1875, and his youngest daughter, Ann, married John Thomas Hawley, son of William Hawley in 1884. It is interesting to find these two sisters living next door to each other in their early married life. I was also very puzzled by the extremely low rent paid for these well-built substantial houses by the Gannons and the Hawleys, — for I knew from my work on my maternal grandparents and great grand-parents that at that time, 1884, rents of fifteen pounds per annum were being paid for only slightly larger houses, else-where in Holyhead. It was only during the last three months that I learned from documents among the Hawley papers that the rent of £2 per annum was in fact ground rent. The papers show that William Hawley (1827-1887) of Eccleshall, Staffordshire, had signed an agreement to lease a piece of land on the North West side of Porthdafarch Road for 99 years, the ground rent being £2 per annum. The document is signed by Edward Edwards, Estate Agent to Lord Stanley of Alderley and the houses are to be completed by November 12th, 1849.

Specifications of the proposed houses are laid down and clauses state that outside walls were to be two feet thick, the timber was to be of good quality pine, a slate roof, good paving in front of the houses. One can easily see why, though built in 1849, they are still in good condition.

These years were, of course, the days of the new railway, and William Hawley was granted a licence to make his first house an inn. He therefore became the innkeeper at the new Railway Inn. Among the Hawley papers are all the licences renewed year after year, until the date of his death. There are also receipts for duty paid to the Collector of Customs on the wine and spirits bought. After his death, the Railway Inn became a dwelling house and there his son, John Thomas Hawley, lived with his wife, Ann. They were succeeded there by their younger daughter, Ann and her husband, W. Henry Matthews. In 1948, ninety-nine years after the signing of the original lease Ann Matthews (Cousin Annie) now a widow, paid the sum of money required to retain the house as her own freehold property, and today her younger daughter lives there.

The Gannons had rented their house from William Hawley, paying the ground rent to the Penrhos Estate, and so had William Hughes, in the years 1851-1856. The Gannons later moved to London Road, and both Gannons and Hawleys rented allotment gardens, the Hawleys renting two, though the Gannons had a very much larger family, — eight children, while the Hawleys had two daughters, Ellen Jane and Ann Elizabeth. Cousin Annie's descendants are, of course, very well-known to us —each succeeding generation having kept in touch with the other.

Grace and Clifford Ballyn do not appear in the Penrhos Rental lists. The addresses which appear in their family Bible, as the birth of each child is recorded, begin in Market Street where their eldest son, Richard James Ballyn, was born in 1873; 15 Thomas Street, where the second son, Clifford Paulin was born, two infants who survived only a few weeks and then my father, William Ballyn, in 1877. Their next home was at 2 Church Terrace, but Clifford James Wyndham Ballyn seems to have lost heart about the arrival, in rapid succession of a very large family, and he never completed the record. However, Do was able to give me precise details of all subsequent births, including her own, and when the family was complete, it became necessary to move to larger quarters at Rostrevor. My great-grandmother

Ballyn had joined them in 1886 and a very large bundle of letters, all written to my eldest Uncle Richard really tells the story of the period 1876 to 1900. These, however, must appear in the story of my grandfather and his Paris - St. Albans ancestry. However, we may include information gleaned from an early Log Book of the National School which the four youngest Ballyns attended.

This Log provided not only information about the family but in its day to day recording, reported events of importance in Holyhead. Week ending January 26th, 1896. " Monday, 22nd January, a general holiday was given in the town to do honour to the Holyhead Volunteers who were leaving that day for Wrexham before embarking for the Transvaal." In the same year on Tuesday, April 2nd, the children were given a holiday that they might have an opportunity of seeing Her Majesty the Queen, as she passed through Holyhead on her way to Ireland. Do remembers this occasion very well; they were all lined up in Tan Lan, each with a small flag to wave, at the appropriate moment. Do stood near the Pelham crossing and remembers the train moving slowly towards the Pier, with a tiny figure in dark clothes, bowing at the window of the Royal Coach. Day to day events in the school are recorded in detail. Visits from the Vicar, Chancellor Briscoe, who gave regular religious instruction. Do also remembers that each autumn he brought large hampers of apples from the orchard at the Vicarage, — then sometimes referred to as the Glebe House. As each child left school she was invited to take an apple from the basket. After 1896 the name of the new Vicar, Canon Walter Thomas, appears. Miss Adeane and the Diocesan Architect, Mr. Harold Hughes, would call, and, of course, the periodical visits of the Inspectors were recorded.

Many of the names I read were those of people, long forgotten, whom I remembered on my visits as a " temporary pupil " between 1907 and 1911. It was interesting to follow the progress up the school of the two aunts, Pauline and Catherine Ballyn, with their cousins, Ellen Jane Hawley,

Ann Elizabeth Hawley and Margaret Gannon. On January 5th, 1901, " Catherine Ballyn began teaching as monitress." The following years she is described as a " candidate " and in 1903 four young pupil teachers are allowed six hours for study each week, Catherine Ballyn being one of them. In December 1905, we learn that Do went to Bangor, to sit for the first part of the King's Scholarship Examination and on April 9th, the following year, was granted leave of absence to sit Part 2 of the Examination at Liverpool University. Do recalled that at Liverpool, she had left a new and treasured pen on her desk during the lunch hour, to find it had vanished during her absence. In great distress she had to use the very inferior pen with a scratchy nib, provided by a rather irritable invigilator. However, she passed her examination and this was duly recorded in the Log.

In January 1896, Grace and Clifford moved house. My youngest uncle, Harry, then aged five, remembers the removal day very clearly, as it was snowing heavily, a rare occurrence in Holyhead. So having arrived at Rostrevor, we may now consider the wheel has made a full circle, for we are back where we began, with Grace and her family at Rostrevor, about nine or ten years before my frequent visits there.

APPENDIX A

After reading the large collection of family letters, I realised that we were not related to Hugh Hugh Hughes, founder of the Hugh Hughes Charity. Our Hugh Hughes was of Ty Mawr Mynydd, born in 1821; he who had returned to Holyhead after some years in Australia, and died in 1893. The father of Grace and this Hugh Hugh Hughes were first cousins, but in true Welsh fashion had referred to him as 'Uncle'. I remembered too, at this point that Do had once told me there was someone in the family who had gone to Australia during the gold rush. This, of course, points to Hugh 1821-1893.

The sum of £10,000 left by Hugh Hugh Hughes 1844-1887 had occasioned a long drawn-out case between the executors of the will and the Attorney-General and the Charity did not begin to operate until 1893, the year our Hugh died. Do, then a small child of seven, had heard talk of both events in the same year and so the mistake had arisen.

Another significant piece of evidence against our relationship with Hugh Hughes of the Charity is that no one in collateral branches of the family had ever heard this particular story. I am glad this mystery has been cleared up.

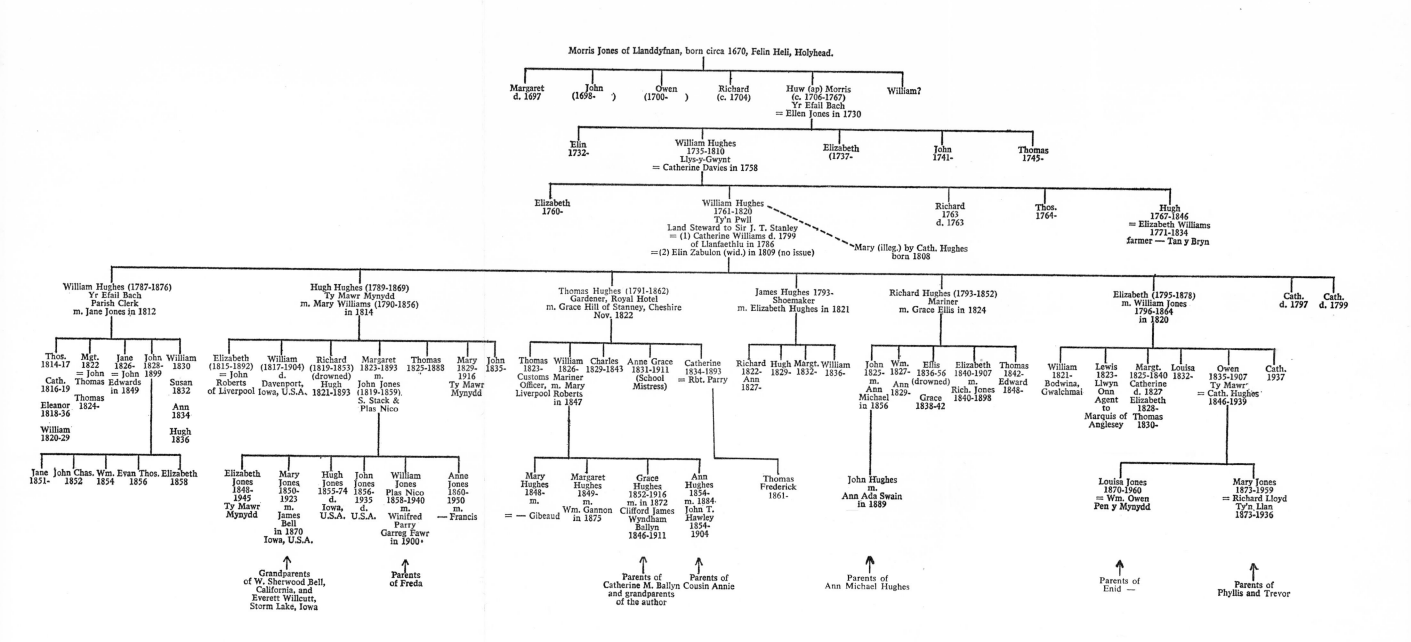

Morris Jones of Llanddyfnan, born circa 1670, Felin Heli, Holyhead.

Margaret d. 1697 | John (1698-) | Owen (1700-) | Richard (c. 1704) | Huw (ap) Morris (c. 1706-1767) Yr Efail Bach = Ellen Jones in 1730 | William?

Elin 1732- | William Hughes 1735-1810 Llys-y-Gwynt = Catherine Davies in 1758 | Elizabeth (1737-) | John 1741- | Thomas 1745-

Elizabeth 1760- | William Hughes 1761-1820 Ty'n Pwll Land Steward to Sir J. T. Stanley = (1) Catherine Williams d. 1799 of Llanfaethlu in 1786 = (2) Elin Zabulon (wid.) in 1809 (no issue) | Mary (illeg.) by Cath. Hughes born 1808 | Richard 1763 d. 1763 | Thos. 1764- | Hugh 1767-1846 = Elizabeth Williams 1771-1834 farmer — Tan y Bryn

William Hughes (1787-1876) Yr Efail Bach Parish Clerk m. Jane Jones in 1812 | Hugh Hughes (1789-1869) Ty Mawr Mynydd m. Mary Williams (1790-1856) in 1814 | Thomas Hughes (1791-1862) Gardener, Royal Hotel m. Grace Hill of Stanney, Cheshire Nov. 1822 | James Hughes 1793- Shoemaker m. Elizabeth Hughes in 1821 | Richard Hughes (1793-1852) Mariner m. Grace Ellis in 1824 | Elizabeth (1795-1878) m. William Jones 1796-1864 in 1820 | Cath. d. 1797 | Cath. d. 1799

Thos. 1814-17
Cath. 1816-19
Eleanor 1818-36
William 1820-29

Mgt. 1822 = John Thomas
Thomas 1824-

Jane 1826- = John Edwards in 1849

John 1828-1899

William 1830
Susan 1832
Ann 1834
Hugh 1836

Elizabeth (1815-1892) = John Roberts of Liverpool
William (1817-1904) d. Davenport Iowa, U.S.A.
Richard (1819-1853) (drowned) Hugh 1821-1893
Margaret 1823-1893 m. John Jones (1819-1859). S. Stack & Plas Nico
Thomas 1825-1888
Mary 1829- Ty Mawr Mynydd
John 1835-

Thomas 1823- Customs Officer, m. Mary Liverpool Roberts in 1847
William 1826- Mariner
Charles 1829-1843
Anne Grace 1831-1911 (School Mistress)
Catherine 1834-1893 = Rbt. Parry

Richard 1822- Ann 1827-
Hugh 1829-
Margt. 1832-
William 1836-

John 1825- m. Ann Michael in 1856
Wm. 1827- Ann 1829-
Ellis 1836-56 (drowned) Grace 1838-42
Elizabeth 1840-1907 m. Rich. Jones 1840-1898
Thomas 1842- Edward 1848-

William 1821- Bodwina, Gwalchmai
Lewis 1823- Llwyn 'Onn Agent to Marquis of Anglesey
Margt. 1825-1840 Catherine 1828- Elizabeth 1828- Thomas 1830-
Louisa 1832-
Owen 1835-1907 Ty Mawr = Cath. Hughes 1846-1939
Cath. 1937

Jane 1851- | John 1852 | Chas. 1854 | Wm. 1856 | Evan | Thos. | Elizabeth 1858

Elizabeth Jones 1848-1945 Ty Mawr Mynydd
Mary Jones 1850-1923 m. James Bell in 1870 Iowa, U.S.A.
Hugh Jones 1855-74 d. Iowa, U.S.A.
John Jones 1856- d. U.S.A.
William Jones Plas Nico 1858-1940 m. Winifred Parry Garreg Fawr in 1900
Anne Jones 1860-1950 m. — Francis

Mary Hughes 1848- m. = — Gibeaud
Margaret Hughes 1849- m. Wm. Gannon in 1875
Grace Hughes 1852-1916 m. in 1872 Clifford James Wyndham Ballyn 1846-1911
Ann Hughes 1854- m. 1884 John T. Hawley 1854-1904
Thomas Frederick 1861-

John Hughes m. Ann Ada Swain in 1889

Louisa Jones 1870-1960 = Wm. Owen Pen y Mynydd

Mary Jones 1873-1959 = Richard Lloyd Ty'n Llan 1873-1936

↑ Grandparents of W. Sherwood Bell, California, and Everett Willcutt, Storm Lake, Iowa

↑ Parents of Freda

↑ Parents of Catherine M. Ballyn and grandparents of the author

↑ Parents of Cousin Annie

↑ Parents of Ann Michael Hughes

↑ Parents of Enid —

↑ Parents of Phyllis and Trevor

APPENDIX B

After the final typescript of the book was complete, I discovered from the Holyhead 1861 Census Returns that the birthplace of Grace, wife of Thomas, the gardener, was Stanney, Cheshire. So we had another Cheshire great-great-grandmother, as well as the elusive Margaret Bell, and no descent from Anthony, the Irishman and his Delilah.

In the throes of a heavy cold, and unable to visit the Cheshire Record Office, I am very grateful to Miss Eileen Simpson whose reply by return of post gave me the results of her search.

In the Bishop's Transcripts for Stoke is found the following baptism —

"April 26th, 1799: Grace, daughter of Thomas Hill of Stanney, farmer, and Ann his wife."

APPENDIX C

Chancellor Briscoe was Vicar of Holyhead from 1857 to 1895. A private notebook of his was kept with the Registers in a safe at the Vicarage; the following entry copied from this book gives the story of the resignation of William Hughes (1787-1876) who had been Parish Clerk for over sixty years.

"1875 Dec. 31st. Wm. Hughes (appointed in 1815) yesterday intimated his intention to resign his office as Parish Clerk. I this day consulted Hon. W. O. Stanley as to what had best be done. At his suggestion I requested Wm Hughes to retain the office & name a deputy, naming to him (as I did to Mr. Stanley & with his approval) Rob. Roberts printer. R. Trevor Parry of Bryngola, Senior Churchwarden (ye other being ill & unable to attend to business) approved of the above. I consequently sent for Rob. Roberts & read him the following, viz., 'Holyhead, 31st. Dec. 1875. Wm. Hughes with the consent of ye Vicar & Senior Churchwarden appoints you his deputy as Parish Clerk. You will receive the £7-10/- per annum paid to him hereto for serving that office & ye Clerk's fees for weddings & funerals which are generally what the parties like to give'."

N.B. (added to foregoing document) "'Ye proper fees (for ye Clerk) are 3/6 for a Funeral (not a pauper's), 5/- for a Wedding by Licence, 2/6 for a Wedding after Banns; but parties sometimes give more & sometimes less.' I then handed to him ye keys of the Church."

94

INDEX OF PEOPLE

95

96

97

PLACES